1906

THE COUNTRY DIARY
OF AN
EDWARDIAN LADY

Edith Holden

*A facsimile reproduction of
a naturalist's diary*

HENRY HOLT AND COMPANY
NEW YORK

Gowan Bank
Olton
Warwickshire

Edith. B. Holden

NATURE NOTES

FOR

1906

".To sit on rocks ; to muse o'er flood and fell,
To slowly trace the forest's shady scene,
Where things that own not man's dominion dwell,
And mortal foot hath ne'er or rarely been !
To climb the trackless mountain all unseen.
With the wild flock, that never need a fold;
Alone o'er steeps and foaming falls to lean;
This is not solitude: 'tis but to hold
Converse with Nature's charms, and view her stores unrolled."

Byron.

JANUARY

Named from the Roman god Janus, who is represented with two faces looking in opposite directions, — as retrospective to the past, and prospective to the coming year.

Jan.1. New Year's Day

Jan.6. Twelfth-Day. Epiphany

" Then came old January, wrapp'd well
  In many weeds to keep the cold away
  Yet did he quake and quiver like to quell
  And blewe his nayles to warm them if he may;
  For they were numbed with holding all the day,
  An hatchet keene, with which he felled wood
  And from the trees did lop the needlesse spray."

Faerie Queen, E. Spenser.

 MOTTOES

" Janiveer
  Freeze the pot upon the fire "

If the grass do grow in Janiveer
It grows the worse for it
all the year."

"A wet January
A wet spring."

" The blackest month of all the year
  Is the month of Janiveer."

January

Blue Tits

Cole Tit
Great Tit

January

The leaves which in the autumn of the year
  Fall auburn-tinted, leaving reft and bare
  Their parent trees, in many a sheltered lair
Where winter waits and watches, cold, austere,
Will lie in drifts; and when the snowdrops cheer
  The woodland shadows, still the leaves are there,
Though through the glades the balmy southern air
And birds and boughs proclaim that Spring is here."

'Old Year Leaves.' Mackenzie Bell.

"Therefore all seasons shall be sweet to thee,
Whether the summer clothe the general earth
With greenness, or the redbreast sit and sing
Betwixt the tufts of snow on the bare branch
Of mossy apple-tree, while the nigh thatch
Smokes in the sun-thaw; whether the eve-drops fall
  Heard only in the trances of the blast,
  Or if the secret ministry of frost
Shall hang them up in silent icicles,
Quietly shining to the quiet Moon. "

'Frost at Midnight'. S. T. Coleridge.

Dead leaves
of
Elm; Oak;
Beech,
Chesnut, and Sycamore

5.

Water Hen
or
Moor Hen.

JANUARY

Jan. 1. New Year's Day. Bright and cold with hard frost.

5   Great gale of wind and rain from the south-west.

11 Visited a small wood on the canal bank, to get violet leaves. On moving away some of the dead leaves lying beneath the trees, I discovered a Wild Arum plant, thrusting it's white sheath up from the soil. When I removed the outer covering, the pale yellow leaves with dark spots were quite discernable, rolled tightly round each other and beautifully packed away inside the white skin. I noticed that many of the leaf-buds on the Elder-berry bushes had burst into green.

12. Saw several Moorhens feeding on a newly ploughed fields, not far from a pond.

14. Great gale of wind and rain

18. Today I saw a curious Oak-tree, growing in a field near Elmdon Park. From a distance it look-ed as if half of the tree were dead and the other half covered with glossy green leaves. On examination the main trunk and two of the main branches proved to be of a species of Oak, that has mossy acorn-cups and large, deeply serrated leaves, — leafless in winter. Growing out of the crown of the trunk and forming fully half of the tree was an Ever-green or Cork Oak, in full foliage. The join in the two trunks was scarcely perceptable.

JANUARY

Jan. 23. Sharp frost and thick fog in the early morning
The fog cleared off about 9.30. A.m. and the sun
shone brightly. Went for a country walk.
Every twig on every tree and bush was outlined
in silver tracery against the sky; Some of the
dead grasses and seed-vessels growing by the
road-side were specially beautiful, every de-
-tail of them sparkling with frost crystals in the
sunshine.   I saw great flocks of Rooks and
Starlings, down on the fields, and a pair of
beautiful Bullfinches in a Hawthorn bush.
The Gorse was in blossom, till within a week or
two ago, but the sharp frosts of the past week
have nipped off the bloom. The mild winter
has brought out the Hazel catkins, wonderfully
early, the small green flowers are fully expand:
:ed on some of the catkins, and the pretty little
red stars of the female flowers are appearing.
The green leaves are out on the Woodbine too
making little spots of green among the under-
-growth.

Jan. 26. The last few weeks, our own and our neighbours'
gardens have been haunted by a very curious Robin
The whole of the upper plumage, which in ordin:
:ary Robins is brown, shaded with olive green,
is light silvery grey in this bird, so that when
flying about it looks like a white bird with
a scarlet breast. I hear that it was seen
about here last summer, it is so conspicuous,
it is a wonder it has not fallen a victim to
somebody's gun.

8.

Ivy
Hazel-nut catkins
Woodbine. and female flowers

January

Jan. 27. Primroses, Polyanthus, Winter Aconite, Mazereon and Snowdrops
are all in flower in the garden. Every mild morning now
the birds are singing and they continue more or less
throughout the day.

Jan. 29. Today I picked some Daisies in a field and saw some
Yew in blossom. The young Nettles are shooting up and
a number of herbaceous plants are shewing new green
leaves, as — Foxglove, Treacle Mustard, Ground Ivy etc.
The Groundsel is in flower too.
Ploughing, and hedging-and-ditching are going on
everywhere. This has been a wonderfully mild
January.

"Wee, modest, crimson-tipped flow'r,
Thou's met me in an evil hour;
For I maun crush amang the stoure
        Thy slender stem.
To spare thee now is past my pow'r
        Thou bonnie gem.

Alas! its no thy neebor sweet,
The bonnie lark, companion meet;
Bending thee 'mang the dewy weet!
        Wi' speckled breast,
When upward-springing, blythe, to greet
        The purpling east.

Cauld blew the bitter-biting north
Upon thy, early, humble birth
Yet cheerfully thou glinted forth
        Amid the storm
Scarce rear'd above the parent earth
        Thy tender form.

The flaunting flow'rs our gardens yield
High shelt'ring woods and wa's maun shield
But thou beneath the random bield
        O'clod or stane
Adorns the histie stibble-field
        Unseen, alane.

There in thy scanty mantle clad
Thy snowy bosom sunward spread
Thou lifts thy unassuming head
        In humble guise
But now the share uptears thy bed
        And low thou lies."

                    To a mountain daisy   Burns.

"Above all flouris in the mede
Than I love most those flouris
White and rede ;
Soche that men call daisies
In our towne"
                    Chaucer

"Daisies smelless, but
most quaint!"
                    Fletcher

Daisy
(Bellis perennis)

"Daisies, ye flowers of lowly birth
Embroiderers of the carpet earth
That gem the velvet sod ;
                    Clare.

"Wee, modest, crimson-tippet flower"
                    Burns.

"Thee Winter in the garland wears
That thinly decks his few grey hairs
Spring parts the clouds with softest airs
That she may sun thee,
Whole summer-fields are thine by right,
And Autumn meloncholy wight;
Doth in thy crimson head delight
When rains are on thee.

In shoals and bands, a morrice train
Thou greet'st the traveller in the lane,
Pleased at his greeting thee again
        Yet nothing daunted,
Nor grieved, if thou be set at nought
And oft alone, in nooks remote,
We meet thee like a pleasant thought
        When such are wanted.

Child of the Year! that round dost run
Thy pleasant course—when day's begun
As ready to salute the sun
        As lark or leveret,
Thy long lost praise thou shalt regain:
Nor be less dear to future men
Than in old time,—thou art not vain
        Art Natures favourite. "
                    "To a Daisy" Wordsworth

"Daisies, those pearled Areturi of the earth,
The constellated flowers that never set."
                    Shelly

1. Spray of Yew
with male flowers

2. fruit.

3. female flowers
in different stages
(magnified)

The Yew (Taxus baccata)

is generally diœcius, the male and female flowers being borne on different trees. It's poisonous properties reside in the foliage, the fleshy part of the berries being quite harmless, though the seed is injurious. Yew trees live to a great age, some in this country being recorded as a thousand years of age. It is supposed to have been planted by the Druids in their sacred groves. In later days it was planted in the church-yards as a symbol of mourning; and some say to provide bows for the archers.

There is a Yew Tree, pride of Lorton Vale,
Which to this day stands single in the midst.
Of its own darkness, as it stood of yore:
Not loth to furnish weapons for the bands
Of Umfraville or Percy ere they marched
To Scotland's heaths, or those who cross'd the sea
And drew their sounding bows at Azincour
Perhaps at earlier Crecy, or Poictiers.
Of vast circumferance and gloom profound
This solitary Tree! a living thing
Produced too slowly ever to decay;
Of form and aspect too magnificent
To be destroyed. But worthier still of note

Yew Trees
by Wm. Wordsworth.

Are those fraternal four of Borrowdale
Joined in one solemn and capacious grove:
Huge trunks! and each particular trunk a growth
Of intertwisted fibres serpentine
Up-coiling and inveterately convolved;
Nor uninformed with phantasy, and looks
That threaten the profane- a pillared shade,
Upon whose grassless floor of red-brown hue,
By sheddings from the pining umbrage tinged
Perenially -beneath whose sable roof
Of boughs, as if for festal purpose, decked
With unrejoicing berries- ghostly shapes
May meet at noontide; Fear and trembling Hope,
Silence and Foresight; Death the Skeleton
And Time the Shadow -there to celebrate
As in a natural temple scattered o'er
With altars undisturbed of mossy stone,
United worship or in mute repose
To lie and listen to the mountain flood
Murmuring from Glaramara's inmost caves.

February

FEBRUARY

This month derives it's name from the word februare, to purify; or from Februa, the Roman festival of expiation, which was celebrated through the latter part of this month.
In ordinary years there are 28 days in February but in leap-year 29.

Feast Days etc.. Feb. 2. Candlemas day
Feb. 14. Saint Valentine
Feb. 24. Saint Matthias.

"February fill dyke Be it black or be it white."

"All the months of the year curse a fair Februeer."

"If Candlemas Day be fair & bright
Winter will have another flight
But if Candlemas Day be clouds & rain
Winter is gone & will not come again."

"If February bring no rain 'tis neither good for grass nor grain."

"In February, if thou hearest thunder,"
Thou shalt see a summer wonder.

February

"One month is past, another is begun,
Since merry bells rang out the dying year,
And buds of rarest green began to peer,
As if impatient for a warmer sun;
And though the distant hills are bleak and dun,
The virgin snowdrop, like a lambent fire,
Pierces the cold earth with it's green-streaked spire
And in dark woods, the wandering little one
May find a primrose."

'Feb. 1st. 1842.'   Hartley Coleridge.

Fair Maids
. of
February

February

Feb 1. Dull day with slight drizzle of rain in the morning but bright and mild in the afternoon.

2. Candlemas day. Wild and stormy.

3. It says in today's Chronicle that at Dover a Blackbird's nest with two eggs has been found. at Edenbridge a Hedge-sparrow's with four eggs and at Elmstead, a robin's with five eggs.

7. Picked some Dog's Mercury in flower; This is the first to blossom of all the wild herbaceous plants, Daisies and Groundsel excepted.

8. There was a thunder-storm today, with showers of rain, hail and sleet.

9. Snow-storm in the night; this morning we looked out on a white landscape, this is the first deep snow we have had this winter. I swept a space free on the lawn and strewed it with bread and rice. Crowds of birds came. I counted eight Tits at one time on the cocoa-nut and the tripod of sticks supporting it. There were some terrible battles among the Tits this morning. One tiny Blue-cap took possession of the cocoa-nut. sitting down in the middle of it and bidding defiance to all the others. It was very funny to see him squatting in the shell, sparring and hissing at a Great Tit who came at him with open wings and beak. There was a partial eclipse of the moon visible this morning at 5.57. a.m. At 8 oclock in the evening there was a beautiful rainbow-coloured halo round the moon, unusually bright and distinct.

10. Rain and wind from the South-west; rapid thaw :

12. I visited the violet wood again today, the Lords and Ladies are quite up above the ground now; and the Violet roots are sending up little green trumpets of new leaves. The ground in the wood is covered with tiny seedlings of the Moschatel.
I gathered some Gorse blossom on my way home. The Elm trees are just breaking into blossom, and the Willows are showing their downy white catkins, — very small as yet.

13. Snowing all day.

14. Saint Valentine's Day. Sharp frost and bright sunshine.

16.

Unfolding leaves
of
Wild Arum
or Cuckoo Pint

(Arum maculatum)

Willow Catkins

Dog's Mercury
(Mercurialis perennis)

Common
Gorse
or
Whin
(Ulex Europœus)

Mountain gorses, ever golden
Cankered not the whole year long!
Do ye teach us to be strong;
Howsoever pricked and holden,
Like your thorny blooms, and so
Trodden on by rain and snow,
Up the hill-side of this life, as bleak as where
ye grow?

Mountain blossoms, shining blossoms,
Do ye teach us to be glad
When no summer can be had,
Blooming in our inward bosoms?
Ye, whom God preserveth still,
Set as lights upon a hill;
Tokens to the wintry earth that beauty liveth still.

Mountain gorses, do ye teach us
From that academic chair
Canopied with azure air,
That the wisest word man reaches
Is the humblest he can speak?
Ye who live on mountain peak,
Yet live low along the ground, beside the grasses meek!

Mountain gorses, since Linnæus
Knelt beside you on the sod,
For your beauty thanking God,—
For your teaching, you should see us
Bowing in prostration new!
Whence arisen,—if one or two
Drops be on our cheeks,—O world, they are not tears
but dew.
                                        E. B. Browning.

February

Feb. 15. Walking home from Solihull this afternoon I noticed a number of Gnats dancing in the bright sunshine. and I saw two little Shrew-Mice in different places on the bank; who darted quickly into their holes directly they saw me.

16. Heard the Lark singing for the first time this year.

24. Cycled to Packwood through Solihull and Bentley-heath. I passed a rookery on the way, the Rooks were all very busy building up their old nests, and a great deal of chatter they made over it. I saw a little Robin gathering materials for it's nest, at one place on the bank and further on, a Thrush with a beakful of long straws: Everywhere the branches of the Willow bushes were tipped with downy white balls and the Alder-catkins were shewing very red: In the garden of Packwood Hall adjoining the church-yard the borders were full of large clumps of single snow-drops. I brought away a great bunch. The farmer living there brought out a little lamb to show me; one of a family of three born that morning. I held it in my arms and it seemed quite fear-less—poking it's little black head up into my face.
Rode home seven miles, in a storm of sleet and snow.

27. Shrove Tuesday.

28. Ash Wednesday. We have had more winter weather this February than any other month this winter.

The Erd Shrew or Shrew-Mouse, inhabits sub-terranean tunnels, which it excavates in the soil. It feeds upon insects and worms; and it's long, flexible nose is a great aid to it in it's search after food. The Shrew is very impatient of hunger and cannot endure a protracted fast; it is suggested that the many dead Shrews which are found in the Autumn on the country roads and foot-paths, owe their deaths to starv-ation, the worms having descended too deeply into the ground for them to follow, and the insects having concealed them-selves in their winter hiding places. The reason that their dead bodies are not carried off for food by Weasels, Owls etc. probably exists in the strong odour which exhales from the Shrew. In country districts a superstitious fear and hatred was formerly entertained against this pretty and harmless, little animal.

To a Mouse.

Wee, sleekit, cow'rin, tim'rous beastie,
　　O what a panic's i' thy breastie!
Thou needna start awa' sae hasty
　　　　Wi' bickering brattle!
I wad be laith to rin and chase thee
　　　　Wi' murd'ring pattle!

I doubtna, whyles, but thou may thieve;
What then? poor beastie, thou maun live!
A daimen-icker in a thrave
　　　　'S a sma' request:
I'll get a blessin wi' the lave,
　　　　And never miss't!

Thou saw the fields laid bare and waste
And weary winter comin' fast
And cozie here, beneath the blast
　　　　Thou thought to dwell,
Till crash! The cruel coulter past
　　　　Out thro' thy cell.

But Mousie, thou art no thy lane,
In proving foresight may be vain;
The best laid schemes o' mice and men.
　　　　Gang aft a-gley,
And lea'e us nought but grief an' pain,
　　　　For promised joy.

I'm truly sorry man's dominion
Has broken Nature's social union,
And justifies that ill opinion
　　　　Which maks thee startle
At me, thy poor earth-born companion
　　　　And fellow-mortal!

Thy wee bit housie, too, in ruin!
It's silly wa's the win's are strewin'!
And naething now to big a new ane
　　　　O foggage green!
A bleak December's winds ensuin,
　　　　Baith snell and keen!

That wee, bit heap o' leaves and stibble
Has cost thee mony a weary nibble,
Now thou's turned out, for a' thy trouble
　　　　But house or hald
To thole the winter's sleety dribble
　　　　And cranreuch cauld!

Still thou art blessed compared wi' me
The present only toucheth thee;
But och! I backward cast my e'e!
　　　　On prospects drear!
And forward tho' I canna see
　　　　I guess and fear.

　　　　　　Robert Burns.

"Now the North wind ceases,
　The warm South-west awakes,
　The heavens are out in fleeces,
　And earth's green banner shakes."

　　　　　　Geo. Meredith.

20.

Catkins of Aspen (Populus trémula)
Purple Willow (Salix purpures) Goat Willow or Round-leaved Sallow
and (Salix caprea)
Alder (Alnus glutinosa)

MARCH

As in the Roman year, so in the English ecclesiastical calendar used till 1752 this was the first month, and the legal year commenced on the 25th of March. Scotland changed the first month to January in 1599. This month was called Martius by the Romans, from the god Mars, and it received the name 'Hlyd Monath', ie. 'loud' or 'stormy month' from the Anglo-Saxons.

Days of note. March 1st St. David. March 12. St. Gregory
March 17. St. Patrick. March 25. Lady Day.

'A peck of March dust
Is worth a king's ransom'.

"So many misties in March
So many frosties in May."

"March'll search ye, April try ye
May'll tell, whether live or die ye'

"March borrowed from Averill
Three days and they were ill
The first it sall be snaw & sleet
The neist it sall be rain & weet
The last it sall be sie a freeze
Sall gar the birds stick to the Trees."

"March hack ham
Comes in like a lion
Goes out like a lamb."

March

March

"The stormy March is come at last
  With wind, and cloud, and changing skies;
I hear the rushing of the blast
  That through the snowy valley flies.

Ah! passing few are they who speak
  Wild stormy month in praise of thee;
Yet though thy winds are loud and bleak
  Thou art a welcome month to me.

For thou, to northern lands again
  The glad and glorious sun dost bring
And thou hast joined the gentle train,
  And wear'st the gentle name of Spring.

And in thy reign of blast and storm
  Smiles many a long, bright summer day
When the changed winds are soft and warm
  And heaven puts on the blue of May."

                         Bryant.

What did Spring-time whisper?
  O ye rivulets,
Waking from your trance so sad,
Pleased to welcome fisher-lad
  With his little nets,
Speed, for summer's in the air,
Prattle, for the breeze is warm,
Chatter by the otter's lair
Bubble past the wied farm;
Wake the primrose on the banks
Bid the violet ope her eyes
Hurry in a flood of thanks.

Underneath serener skies!
What a revel's coming soon
Fairies trooping o'er the leas,
Making magic by the moon,
Crowned with wood anemones!
What a haunted heart the thrush
Nurses in the blackthorn bush,
Full of splendid songs to sing,
Cheery welcomes of the Spring —
    Spring is come!

                    Norman Gale.

"How sweet the hedge that hides
　　a cunning nest;
And curtains off a patient
　　bright-eyed thrush,
With five small worlds beneath
　　her mottled breast!

Though life is growing nearer
　　day by day,
Each globe she loves, as yet
　　is mute, and still
Her bosom's beauty slowly
　　wears away.

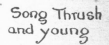

Song Thrush
and young

At last the thin blue veils are
　　backward furled,
Existence wakes and pipes
　　into a bird
As infant music bursts
　　into the world.

And now the mother-thrush
　　is proud and gay
She has her cottage and
　　her pretty young
To feed and lull when western
　　skies turn grey. "

　　　　'A creed' Norman Gale.

Song Thrush's
egg

March

Mar. 1 March has come in like a lamb with a warm wind and rain from the South-west.

4. Glorious sunshine. First warm day of Spring. All the Sky larks up and singing in the blue. Went for a long walk. Found the Colt's-foot and Procumbent Field Speedwell in flower, and down at the edge of a copse, where a little stream ran, on a sunny bank I found a great many Primrose roots with quite large buds in the midst of their crowns of green leaves; the Celandine buds too were very large, another week or two of warm weather will bring them quite out. Everywhere the birds were very active; and such a chorus of voices from every hedge and tree!

6th Tonight a Toad was discovered jumping about in the hall; it must have come in through the garden door which has been standing open all day. Another day of bright sunshine. The leaf-buds in the hedges have been making wonderful progress these last three days of sunshine and the Elm blossom has opened out wide, showing all it's little anthers and filaments. In the morning I visited the field where the daffodils grow; the buds are all standing up above the grass, standing up straight like little green lance-heads among their spears of blue green leaves.

10. Cycled to the withy-beds within half a mile of Bushwood. It was a dull day with frequent showers of rain, so the country looked rather cold and grey. There was no sunshine to light up the ruddy blossom on the Elm and Alder trees. As I cycled between the hedges, I saw numbers of birds carrying on their house-building operations. I went a little out of my way, down the lane to Kings-wood to visit the steep banks where the blue Periwinkle grows. There were numbers of flowers just opening; I only found one blossom fully expanded. The beds of white Violets and the bank where the white Periwinkle used to grow, that I had come to see, were some way off the road, and I had to carry my cycle nearly a quarter of a mile down a steep, muddy ford rough, set thick with thorns, with high banks on each side. On these shelter-ed banks I found numbers of the Small Celandine blossom, and the first flowers of the little Strawberry-leaved Cinquefoil.

26.

Colt's Foot (Tussilogo farfara)   Lesser Celandine. (Ranunculous ficaria)

Young leaves of Hawthorn.   Common Elm. (Ulmus suberosa) blossom.

March

I heard a thousand blended notes
While in a grove I sat reclined;
In that sweet mood when pleasant thoughts,
Bring sad thoughts to the mind;

To her fair works did Nature link
The human soul that through me ran
And much it grieved my heart to think
What man has made of man.

Through primrose tufts in that green bower
The periwinkle trailed it's wreathes,
And tis my faith that every flower
Enjoys the air it breathes.

The birds around me hopped and played,
Their thoughts I cannot measure,—
But the least motion which they made,
It seemed a thrill of pleasure.

The budding twigs spread out their fan
To catch the breezy air
And I must think, do all I can,
That there was pleasure there.

If this belief from heaven be sent,
If such be Nature's holy plan
Have I not reason to lament
What man has made of man?

'Lines written in early spring'. W. Wordsworth.

March.

10. When I got to the bottom of the lane, I set my bicycle against a bank and picniced on a fence.

A beautiful Jay in all the glory of his spring plumage flew screaming across the lane into a spinney of larch trees opposite. He seemed to resent the intrusion of a human being in such an unfrequented spot. I was glad to find the white Periwinkle still "trailing it's wreathes" on the bank; but the flowers were only in bud, and the Violets too, were just uncurling their buds under their fresh green leaves. Among the notes of the numerous birds I recognised those of the Thrush, Blackbird, Hedge Sparrow, Sky-lark, Wren, Great Tit, Chaffinch, Green-finch, Pied Wagtail and Yellow Bunt-ing. The latter was specially conspicious, perched up on top of the hedge with his bright yellow plumage; repeating his cry — one can hardly call it a song — with its last, peculiar, long drawn out note, over and over again. 'A little bit of bread and no che-ese,' the country people liken it to. In Cumberland they say it says, 'Devil, devil dinna touch me-e." This bird is called 'Yeldrin' and 'Yellow Yowlie' in Scotland. I noticed that the white Periwinkle blossoms have five petals, while the blue have only four. I wonder if this is always so.

12. After a wet, windy day, we woke this morning to a regular snow storm, the air was full of whirling flakes, but in the midst of it all I heard a Sky-lark singing.

13. Another heavy fall of snow in the night. The cold has almost silenced the birds this morning. Numbers of them came onto the lawn to be fed; the Starlings and cock Chaffinches look specially gay just now in their spring coats.

14. Hard frost in the morning and bright sunshine. The sun has great power now, and he soon began to make the snow disappear. In the after-noon I went to the Violet wood, and to my surprise I found a number of glowing, purple blossoms in the sheltered glades of the wood. On the way home I found a Robin's nest in the bank of the lane. It was evidently just finished; this is the first finished nest I have seen this year.

20. Went to the Daffodil field again; the buds are just breaking into yellow. Found two Thrush's nests, both in holly bushes; one nest was empty, the bird was sitting on the other. She looked at me with such brave, bright eyes, I could not disturb her, much as I would have liked a peep at her speckled blue eggs. I found some of the green flowers of the Moschatel,

March

" When daffodils begin to pee[r]
With hey the doxy over th[e]
Why then comes in the su[n]
And the red blood reigns in

Catkins of Goat Willow in March.   Blue & White Periwinkle (Vinca minor

'Daffodils, that come before
the swallow dares,
And take the winds of March
with beauty.'   shakespere

ale;
o' the year
winter's pale.'
        Shakespere

Daffy-down-dilly is come up to town,
In her yellow petticoat
And her green gown.

Chaffinchs.   Daffodils
        (Narcissus pseudo-narcissus)

March

House Sparrow
Starling

Wren

Rook

Blackbird

Robin

Song Thrush

Hedge Sparrow

Missel Thrush

Eggs of birds which begin nesting in March.

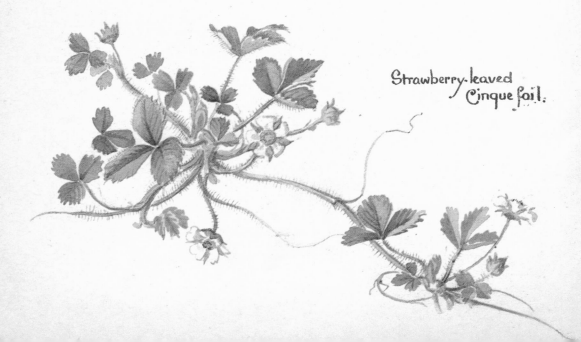

Strawberry-leaved
Cinque foil.

'And hark! how blithe the Throstle sings,
   He, too, is no mean preacher;
   Come forth into the light of things
   Let Nature be your teacher."
                              Wordsworth

"Gloomy winters' now awa'
Saft the westlin breezes blaw,
'Mang the birks o' Stanley shaw,
The mavis sings fu' cheerie, O.

Tow'ring o'er the Newton woods,
   Lav'rocks fan the snaw white clouds
   Siller saughs wi' downy buds
   Adorn the banks sae briery, O."
                              R. Tannahill.

'In days when daisies deck the sod
And blackbirds whistle clear.
Wi' honest joy our hearts will bound
To greet the coming year.'
                              Burns

'Hark! where my blossoming pear
tree in the hedge;
Leans to the field, and scatters
on the clover;
Blossoms and dewdrops at the
bent spray's edge,
That's the wise thrush; he sings
his song twice over.
Lest you should think he never
could recapture
That first, fine, careless rapture.'
                              R. Browning.

"Then the thrushes sang
   And shook my pulses and the elm's new leaves.'
                              E. B. Browning.

Nest and eggs
of Blackbird.

March

Mar 25. Showers of snow and sleet. Quite a heavy snow-storm in the afternoon.

28. Gathered some of the young crimson catkins of the Black Poplar. The last few days have been very cold and dry; with keen north wind, and any quantity of March dust in evidence.

This morning I saw some Frog-spawn which had been brought in from a pond, together with some Caddis grubs in their funny little cases of sticks and straws. One grub looked very smart, he had stuck his house all over with bits of bright green rush and water plant.

Wood Moschatel
(Adoxa moschatel)

31 Cyeled to Bushwood, – a still, grey day, with beautifully dry roads. March is going out like a lamb.
I did not go into the wood, which will be carpeted with Primroses in a week or two's time, but I found quant: =tities of Primroses and sweet Violets, (both blue and white) on the banks of the fields and the roadside. I found the first Dog Violet I have seen in blossom this year at the top of Dick's lane, the Cowslips are only in bud yet; but everywhere the Celandine made the ditches bright; and the Strawberry-leaved Cinque-foil spangled the banks. I saw two Robins' and two Blackbirds' nests, none with eggs in. I saw numbers of sweet birds as I spun along between the hedges. A tiny greenish grey bird flashed across the road, I thought for a minute it was a warbler, but as it emerged into sight again for a moment in the hedge, I saw it was a Golden-crested Wren: I have not seen any of our Summer visitors yet. The Wheatear is the first to arrive in England, I believe, but that bird is not found in this part of the country. The Chiff-chaff is generally the first to put in an appearance here, and he is closely followed by the Willow Warbler.

March has been a very cold month, but dry on the whole: There were two or three bright, genial days in the first week that were like a fore-taste of summer.

Moss-cups.

Violets dim, yet sweeter than the lids of Juno's eyes
or Cytherea's breathe".
Shakespere. Winter's Tale

"As Violets
Recluse and sweet,
Cheerful as daisies
unaccounted rare;
Still sunward gazing
From a lowly seat;
Still sweetening wintry air."
Christina Rossetti

'The snowdrop and primrose
Our woodlands adorn
And violets bathe mid the weet
o' the morn'. Burns.

'Ye Violets that first appear
By your pure purple mantles known'
Sir Henry Wooton.

"And the Spring arose on the garden fair,
Like the Spirit of Love felt everywhere;
And each flower and herb on Earth's dark breast
Rose from the dreams of its wintry rest.
The snowdrop and then the violet,
Arose from the ground with warm rain wet;
And their breath was mixed with sweet odour sent
From the turf like the voice and the instrument. "
Shelley.

Sweet Violet (Viola odorata)

APRIL

The name of this month is derived from the Greek word for 'opening'. In many countries of Europe the first of April has for long been appropriated to a facetious custom for which no satisfactory origin has yet been assigned. To send an ignorant or unsuspecting person on a bootless errand is the great endeavour of the day. In England such an one is designated 'April fool'; In Scotland he is said to be 'hunting the gowk', while in France he is called 'poisson d'Avril' or April fish.

Days of note; Saints' Days etc.

    April 1. All Fools' Day

    April 23. Saint George's Day

    April 24. Saint Mark's Eve.

Mottoes.

    "April weather; rain and sunshine both together."

"When April blows his horn
'Tis good for both hay and corn".

    "An April flood carries away the frog and his brood"

APRIL

" When daisies red and violets blue   And cuckoo-buds of yellow hue
And ladie's Smocks' all silver white   Do paint the meadows with delight."

APRIL

"Oh, how this spring of love resembleth
  The uncertain glory of an April day!
  Which now shows all the beauty of the sun
  And by and bye a cloud takes all away."

                          Two gent of Verona. Shakespere.

"Soon o'er their heads blithe April airs shall sing;
  A thousand wild flowers round them shall unfold;
  The green buds glisten in the dews of spring,
  And all be vernal rapture as of old".

                          J. Keble.

"Come forth, ye blossoms! — over hill and lea,
  A breathe of sweetness wantons with the sea;
  And mid the smiles and tears of tender Spring,
  On dripping boughs I heard the throstle sing:
  Ye cups and stars that strew the fair, green field,
  Ye wings of gold the prickly gorses yield;
  Ye pensive bells to purple pageants born,
  Ye milk-white may-buds of the mantling thorn;
  Ye violet gems and eyes of sapphire blue;
  Wan, flushing wind-flowers and shy elfin crew
  Of every crannied wall, — come forth! — and fling
  Your vernal showers around me while I sing;"

                 'a Song of Salutation: E.M.Holden.

"The young lambs are bleating in the meadows,
  The young birds are chirping in the nest,
  The young fawns are playing with the shadows,
  The young flowers are blowing toward the west —
  Go out, children, from the mine and from the city;
  Sing out, children, as the little thrushes do;
  Pluck your handfuls of the meadow-cowslips pretty,
  Laugh aloud to feel your fingers let them through!"

               The Cry of the Children. E.B. Browning

To the Cowslip.

"Of all spring joys the dearest is
To drink thy breathe again
Freshest of flowers;
The bluebell lights the copse
The primrose paves the glen,
But thy frank beauty over-tops
In open fields
The new-born grass, to meet the kiss
Of sun and wind and showers
and yields
Spring's essence from those fire red drops
That dyed the breast of Imogen.

Sun-freckled art thou as the child
Who kneeleth down to snap
Thy sturdy stem;
And fill with thy pure gold
Her snowy-aproned lap;
White treasury of wealth untold;
Deftly she makes
In bountiful profusion piled
A regal ball of them,
And takes
For sceptre one that high doth hold
His head in pride of April sap.

My earliest love of flowers, how good
To lay my sunburnt face,
In grass so lush,
It shames the name of green;
And fold in one embrace
The clustered heads of all I glean,
And kiss the pure
Warm lips of that fair sisterhood;
Or mid their golden flush
Immure
The splendour of some cowslip queen,
Who reigned apart in loftier grace."

Alfred Hayes.

APRIL

April 1 Very still, grey day. I went to a little spinney to see a large bush of the Great Round-leaved Willow, which is a perfect picture just now; covered all over with great golden catkins, that light up the copse like hundreds of little fairy lamps. The bees were humming all round it, busy gathering the pollen.

4 Third day of bright sunshine. I found another field of wild Daffodils today. The sun has brought out the green leaf-buds on the trees and hedges very rapidly, there is a marked difference in the Sycamore and Hawthorn the last few days; and the Larch is beginning to 'hang his tassels forth.'

7 Another glorious day. Cycled to Knowle. On the way found some Marsh Marigolds and Blackthorn in blossom. The Tadpoles have come out of their balls of jelly and career madly about the aquarium wag= =ging their little black tails. A Gudgeon which had put into the aqua= =rium has made a meal of a good many of them.
Ground Ivy in blossom.

9 Travelled down to Stoke Bishop near Bristol. The low-lying fertile lands round the Avon in Worcestershire were golden with Marsh Marigolds, and as we went through Gloucestershire the banks were starred with Primroses and I saw a good many Cowslips. The Plum and Damson trees were all in blossom.

10 Travelled on, to Dousland on Dartmoor. Primroses thick all along the line

11 Glorious day. Went for a stroll round the fields in the morning and gathered Primroses, some of them the largest I ever saw The Wild Strawberry, Early Vetch Wood Sorrel and Greater Stitchwort are in blossom here. In the afternoon I went up onto the moor to bring home a pony and foal. Both are de= =lightfully picturesque in their shaggy winter coats, and I hope to begin their portraits tomorrow morning.
Up on the moor the world seemed to be made up of sky and gorse, — such acres of fragrant, golden blossom under a sky of cloudless blue. I saw two Wall butter= =flies fluttering about in the sunshine.

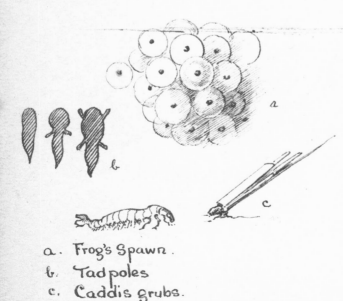

a. Frog's Spawn.
b. Tadpoles
c. Caddis grubs.

I come, I come! ye have called me long,
I come o'er the mountains with light and song!
Ye may trace my step o'er the wakening earth;
By the winds that tell of the violets' birth,
By the primrose stars in the shadowy grass
By the green leaves opening as I pass.

I have passed o'er the hills of the stormy North,
And the larch has hung all his tassels forth
The fisher is out on the sunny sea,
And the reindeer bounds thro' the pasture free,
And the pine has a fringe of softer green,
And the moss looks bright where my step has been."

Mrs Hemans

"And wind-flowers and violets
Which yet join not scent to hue
Crown the pale year weak and new."

Shelley

"Long as there's a sun that sets
Primroses will have their glory
Long as there are violets
They will have a place in story "

Wordsworth

"Now lav'rocks wake the merry morn
Aloft on dewy wing;
The merle, in his noontide bower
Makes woodland echoes ring
The mavis wild wi' many a note
Sings drowsy day to rest,
In love and freedom they rejoice
Wi' care nor thrall oppress'd.

Now blooms the lily on the bank,
The primrose down the brae;
The hawthorn's budding in the glen
And milk-white is the slae."

Burns.

Wood Anemone or Wind-flower
(Anemone membrosa)
Dog Violet (Viola canina)

Primrose
(Primula vulgaris)

APRIL

April 12. Painted the pony and colt all morning in the field. Very hot sun and cool breeze. Saw a beautiful Peacock butterfly and found some Purple Orchis in flower.

13 Good Friday. Went to Burrator and down into Meavy Glen. Everything is very dry; a good storm of rain would bring out many more flowers now. Down in the glen beside the Meavy, the Primroses and Wood-sorrel were very plentiful, growing among the boulders and roots of the trees. The Ash trees are all in flower and some of the young Sycamore trees are in full flower and leaf. While we were resting on the bank of the river, we saw a Heron rise through the trees on the opposite slope and sail away over the wood; the pink and grey tints of his legs and plumage, showing up very distinctly against the brown background of bare trees. We came home across the moor. In many parts the Gorse blossom was glorious, but on Yannadon Down there were great black stretches where the gorse had been burnt.

14. Saw the first Swallow and a Yellow Brimstone Butterfly.

15. Easter Sunday. Another brilliant day. Saw a pair of House Martins, watched some Trout in the Leet and found a Chaffinch's nest nearly finished in a young Hawthorn.

17. Pink Campion in bloom. Walking through the fields, came upon quite a grove of young Cherry-trees in blossom, growing all along the top of one of the banks. The wall-banks that divide the fields here and run along the lanes are beginning to be enamelled with little flowers and ferns, and on the broad tops, crowned with low hedges, the Blue-bells are coming up very thickly. The Blackthorn bushes are a wonderful sight just now, their masses of snowy blossom making a striking contrast with the deep gold of the Gorse.

Miss B. had some lovely Pasque Flowers sent her from Oxfordshire this morning.

19 Bright sun and strong North east wind. Set out for a walk to Lowry. Going over Yannadon Down we saw a young Hare lying in it's form among the gorse bushes. It lay quite still till we had all but trodden on it, when it dashed off among the heather and gorse. Going down the long, steep lane to Lowry, we found some pink Milk-wort, Tormentil and Germander Speedwell in flower on the bank. Opposite the Leatman's little white, thatched cottage we turned off the road, over the Leat, and across the marshy gorse-covered ground that stretches down to the edge of the lake. Here the Gorse and Blackthorn blossom was very fine and in the bogs we found Marsh Violets and the Small Water Crowfoot but there are very few of the bog-flowers out as yet. We also

Sloe or Blackthorn
(Prunus communis)

Spray of budding
Crab-apple

Wood Sorrel
(Oxalis acetesella)

Wall Butterfly (Lasiommata Megaera)
Small Garden White (Peris Rapae)

Marsh Marigold
or Ranunculous
(Caltha palustris)

43.

Swallow (Hirundo rustica)
House Martin (Hirundo urbica)
Pasture Lousewort (Pedicularis sylvatica)

Early Purple Orchis
(Orchis mascula)

Sand Martins (*Hirundo riparia*)
Wild Strawberry
(*Fragara vesca*)

Greater Stitchwort
(*Stellaria major*)
Early Purple Vetch
(*Orobus tuberosus*)

APRIL

April 19. found a good many blossoms of the Lousewort. At the edge of the leat, on the shady side, the icicles were hanging in clusters on the long moss that overhung the water. In Lowry lane just below the quarry I saw one of the prettiest Blackbird's nests I have ever seen; it was all made of moss and placed in the fork of a Gorse bush, growing close beside the road. The mother bird was sitting on the nest and gazed at us with her bright black eyes, but never stirred from her post.

In the after-noon went to Huckworthy Bridge that spans the river Walkham; Down hill all the way. In the meadows beside the river I was surprised to find the blue Alkanet already in blossom just where I found it in July last year, on the over-hanging bank beside the river; The Primroses were thick along the field-banks and I gathered Cuckoo flowers, Red Campion and Bluebells and Bullace; On the way home saw a Horn-beam tree in flower.

20 Today I saw and heard the Chiff-chaff for the first time this year. A number of them seem to have arrived in the neighbourhood, as I saw three different birds, I also saw Stone-chats for the first time on the moor.

22 Went to Bickleigh Vale, — a deep, narrow combe, running down out of the moor, with steep, wooded slopes on either side, and deep down at the bottom the river Plym winding it's way. The ground was carpeted with Anemones and Blue-bells and here and there Primroses, and the tall, handsome plants of the Wood Spurge were very conspicuous with their red stalks and pale green flowers. It was the first time I had ever seen this plant. In one little open glade we came upon a bush of golden Broom flower. The vale was thickly wooded from end to end, — a paradise for birds, among their notes, those of the Great Tit, Chiff-chaff, Robin, and Wren were specially conspicuous. We found beds of the Hairy Bitter Cress and a few blooms of the Mountain Speedwell. We walked four miles through the woods to Plym Bridge at the far end of the Vale. A Water Ouzel skimmed across the river and in under the arch-way of the old, grey, stone bridge, every cranny of which was green with tiny ferns. Then on to Marsh Mills Station, through narrow Devonshire lanes, with high banks hanging with last years' fronds of Hart's tongue and Hard ferns. Here we found the Shining Crane's-bill, Herb Robert; Ivy-leaved Toad-flax; and Treacle Mustard in flower. After more than three weeks drought had a heavy fall of rain at night.

1. Pasque Flower (Anemone pulsatella)
2. Wood Spurge (Euphorbia amygdaloides)

47.

Chiff-chaff (Sylvia hippolais)
Catkins
of Hornbeam (Carpinus betulus)
and
Birch (Betula alba)

Marsh Violet (Viola palustris)
Bilberry or Whortleberry (Vacoinium myrtilis)
Painted Lady Butterfly (Vanessa atalenta)

Evergreen Alkanet
(anchusa sempervirens)

Treacle Mustard or Jack-by-the-Hedge
(Erysimum alliaria)

Brimstone Butterfly (Gonepteryx Rhamni)   Ground Ivy (Nepeta glechoma)

APRIL

April 23. Bright and cold. Saw two live Vipers which had been brought in from the moor; one of them was more than two feet long. The gentleman who had captured them handled them quite fearlessly, he held one up by the back of the neck and forcing it's mouth open with a stick, he showed me the two little pink fangs in the upper jaw.

When on the ground they reared themselves up and hissed, and struck repeatedly at a walking stick placed in front of them.

Watched the sun set behind the hills, from the top of Yanna=don Down. Gorgeous gold and purple clouds near the horizon and up above, clear golden sky. While we were watching it, a Hawk suddenly sailed into the sea of gold above the set=ting sun and remained stationy, poised on quivering wings for quite a long time, then it suddenly dived down into the purple shadows of the plantation just below.

25. Found two more Chaffinch's nests today, and a Hedge Sparrow's nest with four eggs. The Willow Wren has put in his appearance here the last day or two. A native of Dousland showed me a bank covered with gorse and briars, where he said he was sure a Bramble Finch was building, I only know this bird by reputation; so mean to go again and watch for it.

27. Found two Wren's nests, both built of moss, one in the side of a haystack, the other in a bank. Saw a Swift.

28. Showers of hail and sleet.

29 Heavy snow shower in the night; when I looked out this morning the landscape was all white; the distant tors veiled in a mist of driving sleet. Bright sunshine later, with fine effects of sunlight on the distant tors covered with snow.

The Cuckoo has been heard long ago in other parts of the county; but up here on the moors we have not yet heard it.

30. Cold north east wind, with frequent showers, but bright intervals. The latter part of April has been very cold and stormy.

Peacock
Butterfly
and
Larva.

Common Viper
or
Adder
(Pelias Berus)

The Adder is very plentiful in some parts
of England, while in others it is never seen. It's bite is very
venomous and sometimes proves fatal in it's results, which
makes it much dreaded by the country people, who often
persecute the harmless Grass Snake, in their zeal to destroy
the poisonous Adder. The latter may however be readily distin:
-guished by the chain of dark spots which runs along the
spine. The food of the Viper consists of frogs, mice, birds etc.
Like most other snakes it is a very timid creature, always
preferring to fly from, rather than attack a foe.

Wood's Nat. Hist.

'But soft, mine ear has caught a sound; from yonder
   wood it came.
The spirit of the dim, green glade did breathe
   his own glad name.
Yes; it is he! the hermit bird, that apart from
   all his kind;
Slow tells his beads monotonous to the soft
   western wind:
Cuckoo! Cuckoo! he sings again, his notes
   are void of art.
But simplest strains do soonest sound
   the deep founts of the heart."

                              Motherwell.

''Tis the merry nightingale
That crowds and hurries and precipitates,
   With fast, thick warble, his delicious notes;
As he were fearful that an April night
Would be too short for him to utter forth
His love-chaunt, and disburthen his full soul
Of all it's music.'

                              Coleridge.

'You must wake and call me early, call me early, mother dear;
Tomorrow'll be the happiest time of all the glad New Year;
Of all the glad New Year, mother, the maddest, merriest day;
For I'm to be Queen o' the May, mother, I'm to be Queen o' the May.

The honey-suckle round the porch has wov'n it's wavy bowers;
And by the meadow-trenches blow the faint, sweet cuckoo flowers,
And the wild marsh-marigold shines like fire in swamps and hollows gray,
And I'm to be Queen o' the May, mother, I'm to be Queen o' the May.

The night winds come and go, mother, upon the meadow-grass,
And the happy stars above them, seem to brighten as they pass,
There will not be a drop of rain the whole of the livelong day,
And I'm to be Queen o' the May, mother, I'm to be Queen o' the May.

All the valley, mother, 'ill be fresh and green and still;
And the cowslip and the crowfoot are over all the hill.
And the rivulet in the flowery dale'ill merrily glance and play,
For I'm to be Queen o' the May, mother, I'm to be Queen o' the May.

So you must wake, and call me early, call me early, mother dear,
Tomorrow'll be the happiest day of all the glad New Year
Of all the glad New Year, mother, the maddest, merriest day,
For I'm to be Queen o' the May, mother, I'm to be queen o' the May!

The May Queen. Tennyson.

White Dead Nettle *(lamium album)*

Red Dead Nettle
(lamium purpureum)

Wood Crowfoot
(Ranunculous auricomus)

Common Avens
(Geum urbinus)

Wild Pear (*Pyrus Communis*)
Germander Speedwell
(*Veronica chamædris*)

Ladies Smock or Cuckoo flower
(*Cardamine pratensis*)
Cowslip (*Primula veris*)

MAY

The name of this month is of doubtful origin. Ancient writers suggest it to be derived from Maia, the mother of Mercury; to whom the Romans were accustomed to sacrifice on the first day of the month.   May-day is the name given to the first day of the month in England, when, in old days the people went out at dawn to welcome the advent of spring.   May-queens and May-poles were once general throughout the country. The last may-pole erected in London was taken down in 1717. This month is called the Month of Mary, in the Roman calendar.

Feast Days, etc.   May 1.   May Day.

May Mottoes

"Change not a clout
Till May be out."

"Who doffs his coat on a winter's day
Will gladly put it on in May."

"Shear your sheep in May
And shear them all away."

"A cold May and a windy
A full barn will find ye."

"Be it weal or be it woe, beans blow before
May doth go."

MAY

Chaffinch's nest
and eggs.
Hawthorn blossom and Wild Hyacinths.

MAY

May 1. Weather still cold and showery, with bright intervals of sunshine.
Travelled up to Bristol. The country is looking much more beautiful than when I came through it three weeks ago. The Primroses are still thick on the banks, the hedges are all green, many of the Apple orchards in blossom; and the Oaks showing the first signs of golden, bronze foliage. In Somerset the meadows were yellow with cowslips, these flowers are not found in Devon, except on the northern borders of the county; farmers will tell you the soil is 'too good' for them. The Nightingale is also a stranger to Devonshire. One reason I have heard given is, that the insects they chiefly feed on, are not found there, I think this is likely to be the true explanation, as otherwise this flowery, fertile corner of England would seem to be a very paradise for them.

2. Travelled back to Warwickshire; slightly warmer, with continuous rain.

3. Warm south west wind, with heavy fall of rain. Gathered some wild Pear blossom and the first Cowslips I have picked this year. Saw two hen Blackbirds sitting on their nests,—one in a hollow tree. The Crab-apple is only in bud here yet, as are the Wild Hyacinths

4. Heard the Cuckoo.

5. I saw a pair of White-throats today down Widney lane, they were evidently rivals, and were chasing each other through the bushes, singing loudly all the time. By the Blythe I saw a very handsome pair of Black-headed Buntings. In the meadows alongside the stream there was a fine display of Marsh Marigolds and "Ladies Smocks, all silver white." Here I gathered the Corn Crowfoot and Cross Wort Bedstraw.

7. Weather very close and sultry. I discovered a most carefully hidden Robin's nest today in a marshy spinney in Elmdon Park. I was stooping down to gather some cowslips, when a robin fled out over my hand, from under the roots of an Alder Tree, growing close beside me.; it was quite a small tree, supported by four strong roots, which held it up clear of the ground, forming an arch-way. In this cavity, right under the centre of the tree was placed the nest, which contained five eggs. The Crab-apple trees and bushes are looking very beautiful now; covered with pink blossom and crimson buds.

'And after April
When May follows
And the white-throat builds
And all the swallows.'
R.B.

Crab.apple (Pyrus malus)
and
White.throats and nest.

MAY

'Then came faire May, the fairest mayde on ground;
Deckt all with dainties of her seasons pryde.
And throwing flowers out of her lap arounde;
Upon two Brethren's shoulders she did ride;
The Twins of Leda, which on eyther side,
Supported her like to their soveraine queene.
Lord! How all creatures laught when her they spide;
And leapt and daunc't as they had ravish't beene!
And Cupid selfe about her fluttered all in greene.'

Spenser

'While Earth herself is adorning
This sweet May morning,
And the children are culling
On every side
In a thousand valleys far and wide,
Fresh flowers; while the sun shines warm
And the Babe leaps up on it's mother's arm —

Then sing ye Birds, sing, sing a joyous song
And let the young lambs bound as to the tabor's sound
We in thought will join your throng
Ye that pipe and ye that play
Ye that through your hearts today
Feel the gladness of the May.'

'Ode.' *W. Wordsworth.*

Red Campion
(Lychnis diurna)
Wild Hyacinth
(agraphis nutans)
Wild Beaked Parsley
(Anthriscus sylvestris)

MAY

May 9 The Common Avens, Bugle, and Plantain are in flower, and some of the Oaks are hanging out their long tassels of blossom.
I saw a Moorhen's nest today, it was placed on the stump of an old Alder tree, at the edge of a pond, just out of reach of the bank. The nest was built of sticks and pieces of dead reed and contained one egg. I brought home a big bunch of Blue-bells, Red Campion, and Wild Beaked-Parsley, the latter is showing its white umbels of blossom in every hedge-row.

May 11. Saw a dead Hedge-hog curled up by the roadside.

12 Went to Stratford on Avon, and walked to Shottery across the meadows. On the way I gathered Hawthorn blossom from the hedges, and saw fields yellow with Buttercups and banks of blue Speedwell. The Dandelions were a wonderful sight along the railway cutting.

14. Visited the violet-wood this evening; it is quite green and shady there now, as most of the trees are Firs and Sycamores and the latter are in full leaf. The ground was covered with Wild Arums, all in flower, — their pale green spathes gleaming out very conspicuously against the red earthen banks where the rabbits burrow. Some of the sheathes were spotted and I found one deep, reddish purple in colour. The large, handsome green leaves that were so beautiful in the early spring, are now beginning to wither away, as the flowers attain maturity.
I noticed the flower just coming on the Beech; scarcely disting: -uishable from the tender green of the foliage. Oak-apples are plentiful now on the Oak-trees.

16. After a week of warm, growing weather, which has brought out the flowers and foliage wonderfully, we have returned to cold north winds and hail-storms. This morning we had a heavy thunder storm, although there was a cold north east wind blowing. This afternoon I went to gather Cuckoo-pints for my drawing-class. Going through the wood I picked up a Thrush's egg, lying on the ground under the trees. Some of the Horse-Chesnut trees are a mass of white blossom

19. On my way back from Knowle this morning I made a halt at Widney. I saw the Reed Buntings again by the Blythe, I think they must have their nest there. There are quite a number of new flowers in bloom in the marsh by the river, since I passed a fortnight ago. Instead of the unbroken patches of golden King-cups, the marsh is now white with the pretty flowers of the Large-flowered Bitter Cress

"Whoever lives true life will love true love.
I learnt to love that England. Very oft,
Before the day was born, or otherwise
Through secret windings of the afternoons,
I threw my hunters off and plunged myself
Among the deephills, as a hunted stag
Will take the waters, shivering with the fear
And passion of the course. And when at last escaped,
So many a green slope built on slope
Betwixt me and the enemy's house behind,
I dared to rest, or wander, in a rest
Made sweeter by the step upon the grass,
And view the ground's most gentlen dimplement
(As if God's finger touched, but did not press
In making England) such an up and down
Of verdure, nothing too much up or down,
A ripple of land, such little hills, the sky
Can stoop to tenderly, and the wheatfields climb;
Such nooks of valleys lined with orchises,
Fed full of noises by invisible streams;
And open pastures where you scarcely tell
White daisies from white dew, – at intervals
The mythic oaks and elm-trees standing out
Self-poised upon their prodigy of shade, —
I thought my father's land was worthy too
Of being my Shakespeare's. "

'Aurora Leigh.' E.B. Browning.

"O velvet bee, you're a dusty fellow;
  You've powdered your legs with gold!
O brave marshmary buds, rich and yellow;
  Give me your money to hold!

O columbine, open your folded wrapper,
  Where two twin turtle-doves dwell!
O cuckoo-pint toll me the purple clapper
  That hangs in your clear green bell!"

Jean Ingelow.

Common Garlic
(*Allium ursinum*)

Wild Arum,
Cuckoo Pint,
or
Lords and Ladies
(*Arum maculatum*)

MAY

May 19 I also gathered the Yellow Weasel Snout, Lady's Mantle, Field Scorpion Grass and the Garlic, the latter just breaking through it's green sheathe. The hedge-rows are haunted by young fledge=lings; chiefly Blackbirds and Thrushes. I saw one precocious young Robin trying to capture a worm, nearly three times as long as itself. Have seen two queen Wasps this week.

22. Holly, Maple and Mountain Ash in flower.

26. Walking through the fields today I gathered the pretty little Yellow Heartsease; growing among the grass and clover; this species is not nearly so beautiful as the Mountain Pansy with it's richly tinted petals of purple and yellow, which grows plentifully on many upland pastures and hillsides in the mountainous parts of Britain. I also picked the Blue Field Madder, and Pink Clover in blossom

29. Saw some Dog Daisies in flower on the railway bank. My sister brought home some beautiful White Meadow Saxifrage she had picked in some fields near Hatton.

Common Earth Nut, Fumitory and Black Meddick in flower.

May has been a cold, stormy month.

Blossom of Holly
and
Maple

Flower
of the Beech
(Fagus sylvatica)

Oak-blossom
and Oak-apple
(Quercus robur)

Flower
of the Sycamore
or Plane-tree
(Acer pseudo-platanus)

67.

"More pleasant far to me the broom
That blows sae fair on Cowden Knowes
For sure sae sweet, sae soft a bloom;
Elsewhere there never grows."
Scotch Song

Full-flowered, and visible on every steep,
Along the copses runs in veins of gold.'
W. Wordsworth.

It's branches are arrayed in gold
It's boughs the sight in winter greet
With hues as bright; with leaves as green
As summer scatters o'er the scene.
*   *   *   *
An angel mid the woods of May
Embroidered it with radiance gay—
That gossamer with gold bedight—
Those fires of God —those gems of light."
From the Welsh of
Dafydd ap Gwillym

The Welsh sometimes call this plant —
'Melynog-y-waun',-'Goldfinch of the meadow.'
Formerly called 'Planta Genista', it was the badge
of a long race of British Kings, the Plantaganets.

Common Broom
(Sarothamnus scoparius)

Meadow Buttercup
(*Ranunculous acris*)
Common Bugle (*Ajuga reptans*)
Yellow Heartsease (*Viola tricolor*)

Large Flowered Bitter Cress
(*Cardamine amara*)
Yellow Weasel Snout (*Galeobdolen luteum*)

May or Hawthorn
(Crataegus oxycantha)

'Among the many buds proclaiming May
Decking the fields in holiday array,
 Striving who shall surpass in braverie;
 Marke the faire flowering of the hawthorne tree
 Who finely clothèd in a robe of white,
 Fills full the wanton eye with May's delight."
                                                Chaucer

'Hedgerows all alive,
  With birds and gnats and large white butterflies
  Which look as if the May flower had caught life
  And palpitated forth upon the wind."
                                        E. B. Browning.

2.

Large Garden White Butterfly
(Pieris Brassicae)

Blue Field Madder
(Sherardia Arvensis)

2. White Meadow Saxifrage
(Saxifraga granulanis)

Herb Robert
(Geranium Robertianum)

JUNE

Willow Warbler
feeding young.

JUNE

In the old Latin calendar June was the fourth month. Ovid states that this month received it's name in honour of Juno, other writers connect the term with the consulate of Junius Brutus. Probably however it has an agricultural reference, and originally denoted the month in which crops grow to ripeness. The Anglo Saxons called it 'the dry month,' also, 'midsummer month' and in contradistinction to July, 'the earlier mild month.' The summer solstice occurs in June.

Enc. Brit.

Saint's Days etc.   June 11. Saint Barnabas.
June 24. Midsummer Day (Nativity of St. John the Baptist)

June 29. Saint Peter.

June Mottoes.

'Mist in May and heat in June
  Bring all things into tune.'

'A dripping June keeps all in tune'

"June damp and warm   'Barnaby bright (June 11)
  Does the farmer no harm"   All day and no night."

'St. Barnabas, mow your first grass."

JUNE

June 1   North-west wind. Heavy thunder-storms morning and afternoon.

2.   I saw the Yellow Bitter Cress in flower in the marsh at Widney To day. Many of the meadows are golden with Buttercups, and some of the fields are showing quite red, where the Sorrel is coming into flower.

3.   Bright and sunny; the first summer's day we have had.

4.   Whit Monday. Another summer day. Gathered the Greater Celandine and saw the Brooklime and Yellow Rattle in flower.

5   Glorious day, with cloudless sky and bright sunshine all day long.

6.   Another glorious June day. Drove with a large party to Yarningale Common, through Knowle, Baddesley Clinton, Wroxall and Shrewley. The common was covered with short grass and furze bushes and smelt deliciously of Thyme, though we found none quite in flower. There were any number of little flowers growing on the turf, quantities of purple and red Milkwort, Tormentil, Meadow Lousewort, Heath Bedstraw and two species of Vetch and two of Speedwell. There were great numbers of birds, chiefly Linnets and Warblers, flitting about among the furze, I also noticed a pair of Whin-chats and some Tit-larks. We discovered eight bird's nests in the patches of gorse and bramble, – a Yellow Hammers', two Linnets', a White-throat's, a Willow Warbler's, – a Greenfinch's and two Thrush's. Most of the nests had young ones in, but the Yellow Hammer's contained four eggs. There were a good many Small Heath butterflies, flying about the common, and Meadow Browns and Garden Whites were plentiful. The only other butterfly I saw was the Orange-tip.

8.   Cycled through Widney, I gathered the Lesser Spearwort in the marsh there, also Ragged Robin. All the Buttercups are now in flower – the Meadow, – Bulbous and Creeping varieties. There is a wonderfully large crop of Oak-apples on the Oaks this year, I never remember to have seen so many; and the foliage on many of the Oak-trees is quite covered with small green Cater-pillars. The Oak-apple or Oak-gall is formed by a small insect; – the Gall Wasp (Cynips) which thus provides shelter and sustenance for its larva. The transformation from the larval state are completed within the gall, from which the perfect insect tunnels its way out. The formation of the gall appears to be caused by some irritating fluid or virus, secreted by the female insect, and deposited with her egg in the puncture made in the branch.

Milkwort (*Polygala vulgaris*)
Tormentil (*Potententilla tormentilla*)
Smooth Heath Bedstraw (*Galium saxatile*)
Small Heath Butterfly
(*Cœnonympha Pamphilus*)
Meadow Brown Butterfly.
(*Hipparchia janira*)

JUNE

'And after her came jolly June, arrayd,
  All in green leaves, as he a player were;
  Yet in his time he wrought as well as playd,
  That by his plough-yrons mote right well appeare;
  Upon a Crab he rode, that did him beare
  With crooked, crawling steps an uncouthe pase,
  And backward yode, as bargemen wont to fare
  Bending their force contrary to their face;

Spenser.

'A cloudless sky, a world of heather,
  Purple of foxglove, yellow of broom;
  We two among it, wading together;
  Shaking out honey, treading perfume.
  Crowds of bees are giddy with clover,
  Crowds of grasshoppers skip at our feet,
  Crowds of larks at their matins hang over,
  Thanking the Lord for a life so sweet."

Jean Ingelow.

'Why will your mind for ever go
    To meads in sunny Greece?
  Our song-birds have as fine a flow,
    Our sheep as fair a fleece;
  Among our hills the honey-bee,
    And in the leaning pear—
  I tell you there is Arcady
    In leafy Warwickshire.'

Norman Gale.

Orange-tip Butterfly
(Euchloë Cardimines)

Oxe-eye Daisy
(Chrysanthemum leucanthemum)

Purple Clover
(Trifolium pratense)

White or Dutch Clover
(Trifolium répans)

Meadow Fox-Tail Grass
(Alopecurus pratensis)

JUNE

June 8. I saw an Owl tonight, flying across the gardens at the back of the St. Bernard's Road. This is the first one I have seen at Olton.

9 G. brought in some blossoms of the Dusky Cranesbill today. She picked them on the bank of a lane near Sheldon. In all probability the seed of the plant had been carried there from some garden, as this plant is very rare in it's wild state.

12 Silver-weed, Wood Sanicle, Rough Hawk-bit, Small Hairy Willow-herb and Comfrey in blossom. The Wild Service-tree has been in flower for some weeks. This is the eleventh day of bright sunshine without rain.

13 I gathered some Figwort and Celery-leaved Crowfoot this afternoon in a ditch in Elmdon Park, Also found the Bittersweet, Black Bryony and Creeping Cinquefoil in flower. It had been gloomy all morning and before I reached home a heavy storm of rain came on, very grateful after the long drought.

14. Wild Guelder Rose, Elderberry and Wild Angelica in blossom.

Wild Guelder-Rose
(Viburnum opulus)

Lesser Spearwort
(*Ranunculous flammula*)

Brooklime
(*Veronica beccabunga*)

Dusky Cranes-bill
(*Geranium phæum*)

Figwort (*Scrophularia
nodosa*)

79.

'The pleachèd bower'
Where honeysuckles, ripened by the sun,
Forbid the sun to enter.'
'Much Ado' Shakespeare

'All twinkling with
The briar-rose f...

'For the Rose, ho, the Rose! is the eye of the flowers,
Is the blush of the meadows that feel themselves fair,
Is the lightning of beauty that strikes thro' the bowers,
On pale lovers who sit in the glow unaware.
Ho, the Rose breathes of love! ho, the Rose lifts the cup
To the red lips of Cypris invoked for a guest!
Ho! the Rose, having curled it's sweet leaves for the world,
Takes delight in the motion it's petals keep up
As they laugh to the wind, as it laughs
from the west!'
E.B.B. Trans. from Sappho

Dog Roses (Rosa canina)
Honeysuckle (Lonicera caprifolium)

w drop's sheen
streamers green'.
Scott

JUNE

'The evening comes, the fields are still,
The tinkle of the thirsty rill
  Unheard all day ascends again;
Deserted is the half-mown plain,
  Silent the swathes! the ringing wain,
The mower's cry, the dog's alarms,
All housed within the sleeping farms!
The business of the day is done,
The last-left hay-maker is gone.
And from the thyme upon the height,
And from the elder-blossom white,
And pale dog-roses in the hedge,
And from the mint plant in the sedge,
In puffs of balm the night-air blows
The perfume which the day fore-goes.
And on the pure horizon far,
See, pulsing with the first-born star,
The liquid sky above the hill!
The evening comes, the fields are still.'

                              Matthew Arnold.

Creeping Cinquefoil
(*Potentilla reptans*)

Black Bryony
(Tamus communis)
Wild Service Tree
(Pyrus terminalis)

83.

Yellow Iris or Flag
(Iris Pseud-acoris)

Demoiselle Dragon-fly (female)
(Calepteryx splendens)

JUNE

June 15 The birds still sing morning and evening, but there is not nearly such a full choir as there was a month ago.
The cares and responsibities of large families of hungry fledgelings make too many demands on the time and attention of the anxious parents.
It is very pretty to see the House Martins sitting in the roadway, collecting mud for their nests. Their short feathered legs look as if they had little white socks on.
I was quite surprized to come upon a bank of beautiful purple Fox-gloves today, – fully out. These are the first I have seen in flower.

16. Saw the first Wild Rose in bloom, – a fine pink one, on the top of a high hedge.; also Blackberry in blossom. The Roses and Honeysuckle are full of bud, but they are late in bloom this year, owing to the long spell of cold weather

2 Saw the first field of grass down, and cutting-machines at work in several clover-fields: Cow-Parsnip and Birds-foot Trefoil in flower.

23 Cycled through Widnay: The Yellow Irises are out in the marsh there now, and at the edge of the stream I found the large blue Water For-get-me-not. While I was stooping to gather some, a beautiful Demoiselle Dragonfly came skimming across the water and lighted on a bunch of rushes, the next moment it was away again. In the meadow I saw several flowers in bloom for the first time, – Purple Tufted Vetch, Yellow Vetchling, Water-Cress, Slender Tare, Welted Thistle, and in the lanes Hedge Woundwort and Doves-foot Cranes-bill.

Water For-get-me-not.
(*Myosotis palustris*)

Demoiselle Dragon-fly. (*male*)

85.

Fox-glove *(Digitalis purpurea)*
Trailing Rose *(Rosa arvensis)*

JUNE

June 24th. Midsummer Day.

The Cuckoo is beginning to change his tune, a little later he will be saying 'Cuc-cuckoo', instead of 'Cuckoo': There is an old super-stition concerning the Cuckoo's cry in the South of England. If when you hear the Cuckoo, you begin to run and count the cuckoo's crys; and continue running until out of ear-shot, you will add as many years to your life as you count calls. — at least so the old women tell you in Devonshire. There are a good many rhymes about the Cuckoo:

In April Cuckoo sings his lay,
In May I sing all day,
In June I change my tune,
In July away I fly,
In August go I must.'

'The Cuckoo is a fine bird,
She whistles as she flies
And as she whistles, Cuckoo!
The bluer grow the skies.'

June 25th.

Went for a long country walk through Catherine de Barnes, Hampton in Arden, Bickenhill and Elmdon. Everywhere the lanes were fragrant with Wild Roses, and Honeysuckle, and the breeze came to us over the hedges laden with the perfume of the Clover-fields and grass meadows. The grasses of all kinds were lovely, all along the wayside. I found the Meadow Sweet in bloom in many places, Gathered Self-heal and Great Burnet among the meadow grass, and Dog-wood and the white, waxen blos-some of the Trailing Rose from the hedges. We picniced under the hedge, with pink and white Clover bloom and tall grasses nodding round our heads, while a pair of excited Robins chattered and fluttered in the bushes round us, evidently very curious as to what we were about, down in their field-corner. Saw a great number of beautiful little Dragon-flies, — pale blue, with black markings, at a wayside pond, and Yellow Water-Lillies in full bloom on Elm-don Park pool!

June 28. Second day of continuous rain; Earth-quake shocks are recorded in this morning's papers, as having occurred yesterday in some of the Western counties of England and South Wales; extending from Bristol to the Mumbles.

June 30 Scarlet Poppy, Sow Thistle, Plume Thistle and Wild Mignonette in flower.

June has been a very hot month with a large per centage of sun-shine and frequent thunder-storms.

'Then the green rushes — O so glossy green,
 The rushes they would whisper, rustle, shake,
And forth on floating gauze, no jewelled queen,
So rich, the green-eyed dragon-flies would break
And hover on the flowers — aerial things;
 With little rainbows flickering on their wings'.
                              Jean Ingelow.

Great Burnet
(sanguisorba officinalis

Beaked Sedge and Common Rush.   Ragged Robin (Lychnis flos-cuculi)

JULY

July, the seventh month in our calendar, was originally the fifth month of the year, and as such was called by the Romans Quinctilis. The later name of Julius was given in honour of Julius Cæsar, who was born in the month. The Anglo-Saxons called July, 'Mæd-monad,' or 'Mead-month,' from the meadows being then in bloom, and 'Æftera Lida,'—'the latter mild month,' in contradistinction to June, which they named 'the former mild month.'

Days of Note.

July 3. Dog Days begin.
July 15. Saint Swithin.
July 25. Saint James.

July Mottes.

"St Swithin's Day, if it do rain,
For forty days it will remain
St. Swithin's Day an it be fair
For forty days t'will rain nae mair."

"A swarm of bees in May is worth a load of hay,
A swarm of bees in June is worth a silver spoon,
A swarm of bees in July is not worth a fly."

"In July shear your rye."

JULY

"Then came hot July, boyling like to fire,
   That all his garments he had cast away:
   Upon a Lyon raging yet with ire
   He boldly rode, and made him to obaye:
   Behinde his backe a sithe, and by his side
   Under his belt he wore a sickle circling wide."

Spenser.

"The cushat's cry for me;
The lovely laughter of the wind-swayed wheat,
The easy slope of yonder pastoral hill,
The sedgy brook where by the red kine meet,
And wade, and drink their fill." Jean Ingelow

"Yellow with birdfoot-trefoil are the grass glades;
   Yellow with cinquefoil of the dew-gray leaf;
   Yellow with stonecrop; the moss-mounds are yellow;
Blue-necked the wheat sways, yellowing to the sheaf.
Green-yellow, bursts from the copse the laughing yaffle;
   Sharp as a sickle is the edge of shade and shine.
Earth in her heart laughs, looking at the heavens,
Thinking of the harvest, I look and think of mine."

'Love in the Valley.' G. Meredith.

JULY

White Water Lily
(Nymphæa alba)
Great Dragonfly
(Ictinus pugnax)

JULY

1 Fine, but dull, with breeze from the north west.

6. Third day of bright sunshine and fifth without rain. Miss F. gave me some Bee Orchids this after-noon which she had gathered, growing wild in Berkshire.

7 Cycled to Knowle, through Widney. The hedges are a tangle of wild flowers now. There is a fine show of wild roses, both the earlier Dog Roses and the later white, trailing variety are in full bloom. In many places the hedges are festooned with wreaths of Black Bryony and Honey suckle. The pale pink Blackberry blossom and the large, white masses of Elder blossom are every-where conspicuous. Climbing up the banks to meet them are tall purple Fox-gloves and nodding heads of grasses heavy with pollen, mingled with Purple and Yellow Vetches and Clover blossom. The marsh at Widney is quite blue in some places with the large Water For-get-me-not. and the ditches were lined with masses of creamy Meadow Sweet. I saw hosts of tiny, green Moths fluttering round the Oak-trees, that have been so devastated by their caterpillars this spring, and numbers of Small Tortoise-shells & Meadow-Browns. In a corn-field of growing wheat, I saw a number of blossoms of the Opium Poppy. Their large red and purple blooms made fine patches of colour among the green blades. Had a beautiful white Water Lily given me from the pool at Packwood House.

Bee Orchis
(Ophrys apifera)

11 Went by train to Knowle and walked across the fields to Packwood. Hay-making was going on in most of the fields, but the grass was still uncut in the church meadows. Being low-lying and marshy there were numbers of flowers growing among the grasses. — quantities of the deep, crimson heads of the Great Burnet, Dog Daisies, Self-heal, Yellow Rattle, Knapweed, Spotted Orchis and Yellow and purple Vetches. Picked a great bunch of Quaking grass, and at the little bridge that spans the stream we stopped to gather some of the Branched Bur-reed. Passing through a corn-field I not-:iced that nearly every stalk of wheat had the Small Bindweed Twining closely round it, and here were quantities of Corn Crowfoot with its cur-:ious prickly seed vessels. By the roadside I gathered Wood Germander, Henbit Nettle. — the brightest of all the red nettles —Woodruff, Small Upright St. John's Wort, Perforated St. John's Wort, White and Pink Mallow, Rose-bay Wil-:low Herb, Yellow Vetchling, Greater Trefoil, Small Scabious, and the first Hare-bells I have seen this year. The Privet is all in flower now, and the Lime just expanding its blossoms, after showing its tight, little green balls of buds for many weeks past.

Small Tortoiseshell
(*Vanessa Urticæ*)

Meadow Sweet
or
Queen of the Meadow
(*Spiræa salicifolia*)

Small Upright St John's Wort
(*Hypericum pulchrum*)

Stinging Nettle
(*Urtica Dioica*)

JULY

July 14. Glorious day after a day of heavy rain. On my weekly ride to Knowle, saw the following flowers in bloom since I passed through the lanes a week ago, — Field Knautia, Small Scabious, Nipple-wort, Water Dropwort, Corn Sow thistle, Creeping Plume Thistle and Ivy-leaved Lettuce; as well as several varieties of Hawk-weed. Many of the Oak-trees which were so devastated by caterpillars this year, are producing quite a new crop of foliage.

16. Saw a Blackbird sitting on its nest today, in the top of a high Hawthorn hedge.
It is the caterpillar of the Small Green Oak Moth (*Tortrix viridana*) which ravages the Oak leaves.

21. Cycled to Baddesley and walked from there to Balsall Temple. I knew the wild Canterbury Bell (Creeping Campanula) used to grow by the streams there, years ago, and I was anxious to find it again, nor was I dis-appointed. The tall spikes of purple bells were very conspic-uous, growing in a deep ditch, among masses of Meadow-sweet and nettles, into the midst of which I valiantly plung-ed, though the Nettles met over my head and didn't fail to remind me of their presence. I crossed the meadows to the bank of the little river, where the Purple Loose-strife or Long Purples was just coming into flower. There too I found some of the blue Meadow Crane's-bill. All along the stream were great quantities of Water Figwort and the pretty little Un-branched Bur-reed with its balls of pale gold. The large Water Forget-me-not was rampant everywhere and in one place the bed of the stream was covered with Yellow Water Lilies. I captured two of the blossoms and one of the broad, shining leaves, that were growing near the bank. I saw a beautiful Kingfisher skim across the water There were beds of tall rushes, nearly six feet high, with blue green stems, and knotted clusters of brown flowers, I think they must have been a species of Club Rush. This is a beautiful bit of country, — low-lying meadows with sedgy streams, meandering through them, lined with beds of Water flowers and rushes. I went a mile out of my way, down a narrow lane, to search for the Spreading Campanula, where it used to grow years ago, but all trace of it had disappeared. Along a lane just above Balsall, I came suddenly upon a great flock of Meadow Brown Butterflies, I had seen numbers of them all along the way, but here the air was thick with them, flying hither and thither. One side of the lane was bordered by a broad patch of meadow grass and a steep bank, covered with Hen-bit Nettle and Knapweed and topped

Branched Bur Reed (*Sparganium ramosum*)
Common Flowering Rush (*Butumos umbellatus*)
Spotted Palmate Orchis (*Orchis maculata*)
Rose-bay Willow Herb (*Epilobium augustifolium*)

Red-tailed Humble Bee
(Bombus lapidarius)

Red Admiral
Butterfly (Vanessa At

Lesser Bird's-foot Trefoil
Lady's Slipper or
Lady's Fingers & Thumbs *(Lotus corniculatus)*

Purple Tufted Vetch
(Vicia cracca)
Meadow Vetchling
(Lathyrus pratensis)
Greater Bird's-foot Trefoil
(Lotus major)

97.

Common Nipplewort
(Lapsana communis)

Bitter-sweet
(Solanum dulcamera)

Fine Bent Grass
(Agrostis vulgaris)

Flower of Lime
or Linden Tree
(Tilia Europæa)

Common Bumble Bee
(Bombus terrestris)

Hive Bee
(Apis mellifica)

Privet (Ligustrum vulgare)

99.

Small Bindweed
(convolvulus arvensis)

Couch Grass
Quaking Grass

Silky Bent Grass
Brome Grass

Giant Campanula
(Campanula persicifolia)

Common Agrimony
(Agrimonia eupatoria)

JULY

21. (con.) by a hedge of Privet in full bloom. It may have been the strong scent of the Privet which attracted the butterflies to the spot. On the slope of a dry upland field I gathered the Hemp Agrimony and down at the bottom of a dry marl-pit in a corner of the same field I spied the pale yellow spikes and sea-green foliage of the Great Mullein.

23. Toadflax; Ragweed and Tansy in bloom.

31. Close and sultry. This month bears the highest record for heat of any this summer.

Yellow
Water Lily
Nymphæa lutea)

103.

Great Hairy Willow Herb
(Epilobium hirsutum)

Purple Loose-strife
(Lythrum salicaria)

Meadow
Crane's-bill
(Geranium pratense)

Yellow Toadflax
(Linaria vulgaris)
Common Ragwort
(Senicis jacobœa)

Magpie Moth.

Creeping Plume Thistle
(Cnicus arvensis)

Welted Thistle
(Carduus acanthoides)

Cotton Thistle
(Onopordum acanth

AUGUST

This month received it's present name from the Emperor Augustus, and was selected not as being his natal month, but because in it his greatest good fortune happened to him. As July contained 31 days, and August only 30, it was thought necessary to add another day to the latter month, in order that August=us might not be in any respect inferior to Julius.

(Enc. Brit.)

August 24th   Saint Bartholomew.

Mottoes.

"All the tears St. Swithin can cry
St Bartlemy's mantle wipes them dry."

"St. Bartholomew (August 24th)
Brings the cold dew."

"If the 24th of August be fair and clear
Then hope for a prosperous Autumn that year."

AUGUST

Fairest of months! ripe Summer's Queen
    The hey-day of the year
    With robes that gleam with sunny sheen,
    Sweet August doth appear.
                        R. Combe Miller.

The moor-cock springs on whirring wings
    Among the blooming heather;
    Come, let us stray our gladsome way
    And view the charms of Nature,
    The rustling corn; the fruited thorn.
    And every happy creature
                        Burns.

There is no breeze upon the fern,
    No ripple on the lake;
    Upon her eyrie nods the erne,
    The deer has sought the brake;
    The small birds will not sing aloud
    The springing trout lies still,
    So darkly looms yon thunder-cloud,
    That swathes as with a purple shroud
    Ben-ledi's distant hill.
                      Scott.

AUGUST

AUGUST

Aug. 1.   Warm, bright day with south-west breezes.

   2   Gathered Water Plantain in blossom.

   4.   Went to a corn-field to gather Poppies, but a heavy shower early in the day had dashed most of the blooms.
   Found three different species of Persicaria growing among the corn, and quantities of Hare-bells on the field-banks on the way home.
   Harvesting commenced.

   9.   Travelled up to Carlisle and drove eight miles through Cumberland lanes between banks covered with Harebells, Toadflax, and Hawkweed, crowned by low hedges waving with the long streamers of Honeysuckle and sweet scented Bedstraw. In many places the fields were golden with Ragweed.

   11.   Travelled on to Callander in Perthshire.

   14th   Went to Oban and back by West Highland railway; Quantities of wild flowers all along the route, – on the banks, –Golden-rod, Blue-bells and Heather, and in the bogs and marshlands – Meadow-Sweet, Willow-herb, Trefoil and Knapweed & a small kind of Scabious. The Butterwort is over, as is also the Bog Asphodel.

   17.   Cycled to Aberfoil by Lake of Menteith, and back by Loch Achray, Loch Katrine and Loch Vennachar. Very bright, clear day, with wonderfully fine distant views. On the high ridge of hills between Aberfoil and the Trossachs I found the bright scarlet berries of the Bear-berry growing among the heather, and Sundew in flower. Found some Gentian beside Loch Vennachar.

   23   Went to sketch Highland cattle on the Putting-stone Hill.
   Found numbers of beautiful little purple Hearts-ease growing on the short turf and came upon a big bog full of Grass of Parnassus, in the midst of the heather and Juniper bushes. The berries of the latter are still green.

   24.   Saw several Black-cock on the hill-side.

Greater Water Plantain
(Alisma plantago)

Creeping Loose-strife

Common Red Poppy
(Papaver Rhœas)

Hare-bell
(Campanula rotundifolia)

Mayweed
(Matricaria inodorata)

113.

Sneeze-wort Yarrow
(Achillea Ptarmica)

Devil's-bit Scabious
(Scabiosa succisa)

Common Eye-bright
(Euphrasia officinalis)

Heather or Ling
(Calluna vulgaris)
Cross-leaved Heath
(Erica Tetralix)
Fine-leaved Heath.
(Erica cinerea)

Golden Rod (Solidago vulgaris)
Hips of Villous Rose (Rosa villos

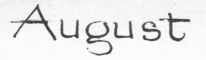

August

Aug. 25. Cycled through Strathyre and Lochernhead to St. Fillan's. at the head of Loch Erne. Hay-making going on in all the valleys, many of which are flooded with the continuous rains. The berries on tree and bush are beginning to make themselves conspicuous, notably the Rowans, Wild Raspberries, (which are very plentiful in the Highlands) and the hips of a species of Wild Rose which has very large crimson fruit. I gathered the first Blackberries at St. Fillans. The road along the North side of Loch Erne is very fine; it runs for six miles close to the edge of the loch, with the water lapping up on one side and steep woods stretching up the hillside on the other. There were many fine trees bordering the road; I saw the finest Larches here I have ever seen.

28   As I was walking across the fields to the cattle today, a Snipe flew up from the grass at my feet, soon after I saw a Curlew alight in the field. There were numbers of Starlings running round about the cattle as they were feeding, follow- =ing the animals all round the field, they seemed to be picking up the insects, disturbed by the animals in browsing

There has been almost continuous rain in Scotland this month, although in England, it has been one of the sunniest months on record.

117.

Red Bear-berry
(Uva ursa)

Bog Myrtle or Sweet Gale
(Myrtica gale)

Grass
of Parnassus
(*Parnassia palustris*)-

Purple Heart's-ease
(*Viola lutea*)

Thrush feeding
on the berries
of the Rowan
or Mountain Ash.
(Pyrus aucuparia)

August

'She lived where the mountains go down to the sea,
   And river and tide confer,
      Golden Rowan of Menolowan,
   Was the name they gave to her.

She had the soul no circumstance
      Can hurry or defer;
     Golden Rowan of Menolowan
   How time stood still for her !

Her playmates for their lovers grew,
     But that shy wanderer,
     Golden Rowan of Menolowan
  Knew love was not for her.

Hers was the love of wilding things;
     To hear a squirrel chirr,
  In the golden rowan of Menolowan
   Was joy enough for her.

She sleeps on the hill with the lonely sun,
    Where in the days that were,
  The golden rowan of Menolowan
   So often shadowed her.

The scarlet fruit will come to fill,
   The scarlet spray to stir,
    The golden rowan of Menolowan,
  And wake no dream for her.

Only the wind is over her grave
    For mourner and comforter,
And 'Golden Rowan of Menolowan'
   Is all we know of her .'

Bliss Carmen.

September

September was the seventh month of the Roman calendar, but is the ninth according to our reckoning. The Anglo-Saxons called it 'gerst-monath', — Barley month!

Feast Days.

September 21.   St. Matthew.
September 29.   St Michael
or
Michaelmas Day

Mottoes   'Fair on September first, fair for the month'.

'Plant trees at Michaelmas & command them to grow
Set them at Candlemas & entreat them to grow.'

'September blows soft,—   'St Matthew
Till the fruits' in the loft.'   Brings cold dew.'

'September dries up wells, or breaks down bridges.'

September

House Sparrows
and
Oats.

September

Best I love September's yellow,
    Morns of dew-strung gossamer;
Thoughtful days without a stir;
Rooky clamours, brazen leaves,
Stubble dotted o'er with sheaves—
More than Spring's bright uncontrol
Suit the Autumn of my soul.'

Alex. Smith.

'The splendour falls on castle walls
    And snowy summits old in story,
The long light shakes across the lakes;
    And the wild cateract leaps in glory.
·Blow, bugle, blow, set the wild echoes flying,
Blow, bugle, answer, echoes, dying, dying, dying.

O hark, O hear! How thin and clear,
    And thinner, clearer, farther going!
O sweet and far from cliff and scar
    The horns of Elfland faintly blowing!
Blow, let us hear the purple glens replying
Blow, bugle; answer, echoes, dying, dying, dying."

Tennyson.

Goldfinch
feeding on
Thistle-seed.

September

Sept 1. Hottest day we have had here yet. This is the third day of bright sunshine. Cycled, through Doune to Dunblane, through well-wooded, rolling country, with low hills and fine, distant views. The road followed the windings of the Teith for a great part of the way. They have commenc=ed harvesting in the Oat-fields

17. Rowed to the top of Loch Vennachar and pic-niced on the shore. The Brake Fern on the hills is be-ginning to turn bronze and yellow. Great quantities of it have been cut and left to dry on the hillside, making great patches of red and brown. None of the trees are turning colour as yet. On the way home we wit-nessed a wonderful sunset across the water. The reflect-ed light on the Eastern hilltops was gorgeous, - all shades of gold and red and brown, deepening into purple and grey shadows at the base of the mountains. There was a curious, gold-brown dust lying all over the surface of the loch, which we thought must be Heather pollen, blown across from the hills.

22. Walked to the Lake of Menteith and back across the hills. Unlike most of the Scotch lochs the shores are flat and marshy and surrounded by large beds of reeds, which are a great resort of Water-fowl of all kinds. The lake is noted for the number of large Pike it contains. The walls of the little inn-parlour on the edge of the lake are hung round with fine, stuffed specimens in cases, that have been captured in its waters. Rowed across to Inchamahone Priory, on one

Juniper berries
(*Juniperus communis*)

Round-leaved Sundew
(*Drosera rotundifolia*)

Seed-vessels
of
Bog Asphodel

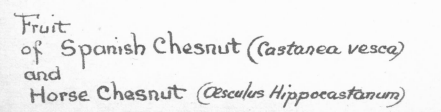

Fruit
of Spanish Chesnut (Castanea vesca)
and
Horse Chesnut (Œsculus Hippocastanum)

September

Sept 22. off the two islands. Here were huge old Spanish Chesnut Trees, supposed to have been planted by the monks, and the largest Nut trees 'I have ever seen; also the Box tree, said to have been planted by Queen Mary. Most of the Chesnut trees were green and vigorous, with wonderful, twisted trunks, and covered with fruit, as were the Nut trees.

The ruined walls of the Priory were green with the tiny Wall Spleenwort; and Hare-bells were waving their purple bells aloft from many of the top-most crevices. Crossing the high ridge of hills between the Teith Valley and the Menteith district we travers=ersed some extensive peat-bogs. The colours of some of the mosses and bog plants were very vivid the orange seed-vessels of the Asphodel and deep crimson, and palest of pale green, mosses being particularly striking. The Heather is all turning brown now,— only a pink bit here and there.

Sept 25. Goodbye to Scotland and back to the Midlands once more.

Sept. 30. Scarcely any of the foliage on the trees is turned colour. Some of the Beech trees are quite bare, the leaves having shrivelled up and fallen off, this is doubtless due to the long drought there has been here.

Weather still continues perfect. Hot sun during the day, cold and clear at night; mist in the mornings.

September

'While ripening corn grew thick and deep,
And here and there men stood to reap,
One morn I put my heart to sleep,
And to the meadows took my way:
The goldfinch on a thistle-head:
Stood scattering seedlets as she fed,
The wrens their pretty gossip spread,
Or joined a random roundelay.'

Jean Ingelow.

Fruit
of
Wild Guelder Rose
(Viburnum opulus)

Fruit
of Dog Rose (*Rosa canina*)
and
Blackberry (

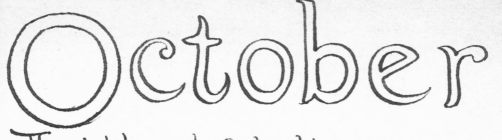

October

The eighth month of the old Roman year.
By the Slavs this is called 'Yellow month', from the
fading of the leaf; to the Anglo-Saxons, it was
known as Winter fylleth, because at this moon
(fylleth) winter was supposed to begin.

Days of note.

    October 18. St Luke.

    October 28. St Simon and St Jude.

Mottoes:

    'By the 1st of March the crows begin to search,
    By the 1st of April they are sitting still,
    By the 1st of May they are flown away,
    Creeping greedy back again
    With October wind and rain.'

    'A good October and a good blast,
    To blow the hog, acorn and mast.'

    'In October dung your field
    And your land it's wealth shall yield.'

October

Yellow-Hammers
feeding in stubble .

October

'Then came October, full of merry glee.'
Spenser

'Calm and deep peace, on this high wold;
And on these dews that drench the furze,
And all the silvery gossamers
That twinkle into green and gold.

Calm and still light on yon great plain
That sweeps with all it's autumn bowers,
And crowded farms and lessening towers,
To mingle with the bounding main.'
Tennyson.

'As yet the blue-bells linger on the sod
That copes the sheepfold ring, and in the woods
A second blow of many flowers appears,
Flowers faintly tinged and breathing no perfume;
But fruits, not blossoms, form the woodland wreathe
That circles Autumn's brow: The ruddy haws
Now clothe the half-leaved thorn, the bramble bends
Beneath it's jetty load; the hazel hangs
With auburn branches, dipping in the stream
That sweeps along, and threatens to o'erflow
The leaf-strewn banks:—Oft statue-like I gaze,
In vacancy of thought, upon that stream,
And chase, with dreaming eye, the eddying foam
Or rowan's clustered branch, or harvest sheaf,
Borne rapidly down the dizzying flood.'
Grahame

October

Oct. 1. Warm, bright day. There are not many wild flowers left in bloom here now; I gathered some Scabious, and Red Dead Nettle today, and saw some White Convol-vulous on the top of a hedge. Blackberries are plenti-ful, and there is a rich harvest of berries of all kinds. I brought in some long necklaces of the bright scarlet berries of the Black Bryony, and some boughs laden with Chesnuts, to paint.

2 Rain and wind from the South-west.

3 The Swifts have all disappeared and for some days I have not seen any Martins flying about. Long before I left Perth-shire, every morning I used to watch the House Martins from my bed-room window, collecting in great flocks on the house-roofs, preparatory to their departure.
There are still some Swallows to be seen, but the great-er number have gone South.
The Robins are beginning to sing again.

5. Today I was watching a number of Sparrows and Tom-tits flutter-ing round, and hanging on to, the heads of the Sunflowers that are all gone to seed in the garden. The birds have evidently discovered that the interstices between the sunflower seeds are a favorite resort of insects, - more especially beetles and ear-wigs. The weather still continues close and showery.

10 Walking through the fields today to Elmdon Park, I saw numbers of the little blue blossoms of the Field Speedwell; these, and Mayweed, Pink Campion and a few belated Blackberry blossoms were the only wild flowers I saw. The Campion continues to show stray blooms all through the winter, whenever there is a mild spell of weather. The Wild-Service trees in Elmdon Park are a gorgeous colour now, - the upper part of the foliage crimson and scarlet and the lower deep orange. A few of the other trees are begin-ning to turn colour, but green is the predominating tone of the foliage as yet. I brought home some of the fruit of the Wild Service

Berries
of Bittersweet
or Woody Nightshade
(Solanum dulcamera)

Hazel Nuts (*Corylus avellana*)
and
Acorns (*Quercus pedunculata*)

Give to me the life I love,
   Let the lave go by me.
Give the jolly heaven above,
   And the byway nigh me.
Bed in the bush with stars to see,
   Bread I dip in the river —
There's the life for a man like me,
   There's the life for ever.

Let the blow fall soon or late,
   Let what will be o'er me;
Give the face of earth around
   And the road before me.
Wealth I seek not, hope nor love,
Nor a friend to know me;
All I seek, the heaven above
   And the road below me.

Or let autumn fall on me
   Where afield I linger,
  Silencing the bird on tree;
   Biting the blue finger.
White as meal the frosty field —
   Warm the fire-side haven —
Not to autumn will I yield,
   Not to winter even!

Let the blow fall soon or late,
   Let what will be o'er me
Give the face of earth around,
   And the road before me.
Wealth I ask not, hope nor love,
   Nor a friend to know me;
All I ask, the heaven above
   And the road below me.

                    R. L. Stevenson.

October

Below is a list of the fruits and berries which I have gathered in this neighbourhood this Autumn. There are other varieties to be found I know in other parts of Warwickshire, but not a large num= =ber.

Wild Pear, Crab apple, Sloe, Bullace, Blackberry, Hips, Haws, Horse-Chesnut, Spanish or Sweet Chesnut, Wild Service Tree, Hazel Nut, Beechmast, Dogwood or Cornel, Elderberry, Bitter-sweet or Woody Night-shade, Black Bryony and Yew.

Of these the berries of the Bittersweet and Bryony alone are poisonous, although the berries of the Dogwood are very astringent and unpleasant in flavour. It is curious that although the foliage of the Yew contains so much poison, the berries are harmless and eagerly eaten by the birds, the only injurious part being the hard seed in the centre, which the birds reject.

I omitted to mention in the above list, the Guelder Rose and the Mountain Ash or Rowan; To these should be added the Holly,—the berries of which are now scarlet and the Privet.—twenty one in all.

Berries
of
Black Bryony (*Tamus communis*)

To Autumn.

Season of mists and mellow fruitfulness!
  Close bosom-friend of the maturing sun ;
  Conspiring with him how to load and bless
With fruit the vines that round the thatch-eaves run;
To bend with apples the moss'd cottage-trees,
  And fill all fruit with ripeness to the core ;
To swell the gourd and plump the hazel shells
  With a sweet kernel, to set budding more,
And still more, later flowers for the bees,
Until they think warm days will never cease,
  For Summer has o'er-brimmed their clammy cells .

Who hath not seen thee oft amid thy store ?
  Sometimes whoever seeks abroad may find
Thee sitting careless on a granary floor,
  Thy hair soft-lifted by the winnowing wind ;
Or on a half-reap'd furrow sound asleep,
Drowsed with the fume of poppies while thy hook
  Spares the next swathe and all it's twinèd flowers;
And sometimes like a gleaner thou dost keep
  Steady thy laden head across a brook ;
Or by a cider-press, with patient look,
Thou watchest the last oozings hours by hours.

Where are the songs of Spring ? Ay, where are they?
  Think not of them, thou hast thy music too. —
While barrèd clouds bloom the soft dying day;
  And touch the stubble-plains with rosy hue,
Then in a wailful choir the small gnats mourn,
Among the river sallows, borne aloft
  Or sinking as the light wind lives or dies.
And full-grown lambs bleat loud from hilly bourn;
  Hedge-crickets sing, and with treble soft
The redbreast whistles from a garden-croft;
And gathering swallows twitter in the skies.

                                        J. Keats

Fruit
of Elder-berry tree
(Sambucus nigra)
and Beech
(Fagus sylvatica)

October

Oct 10th tree and some Acorns, to paint. Looked for Crab-Apples, but could not find any, although the was a quantity of blossom in the Spring. Probably they have all been gathered. The hedges are gay with berries of all kinds, — Hips and Haws, Elder-berries, Bryony, Bitter-sweet, Guelder Rose, and Black-berries, — and the birds were busy, feasting among them. Was caught in a thunder-storm on the way home.

14. Bright and cold, after a week of damp, rainy weather. Walked to Catherine de Barnes to get some Dogwood berries, which I knew were plentiful in the hedges about there. The Hips made a great display all along the route, especially on a wild piece of common land we crossed, covered with Gorse and briars. I noticed great numbers of Finches here, feeding on the berries. Some of the Gorse bushes were in flower; these with the bushes of scarlet Rose-berries, and trailing Black-berry briars, covered with red and yellow leaves, made fine patches of colour in the bright sunshine. I saw some Hare-bells and Sow-thistle in flower, and some Crab Apples on a tree, which I vainly tried to reach. The cottage gardens are very gay just now with Chrysanthemums, Dahlias, and Michaelmas Daisies, and the cottage walls are covered with great splashes of crimson, when the Virginia creeper has turned colour.

16. My sister sent me some lovely crimson toad-stools with white spots, this morning, from Keston Common. Though a good deal damaged by the journey, — all the heads of the toad--stools being severed from their stems, I managed to make a sketch of one or two

21. The last of our summer visitants has taken his departure. About a fortnight ago a Chiff-chaff was constantly to be seen hopping about the Goose-berry bushes in the garden; — the last to leave us, he is usually the first to arrive. But the Tom-tits are returning in great numbers to their old haunts in the garden, which they have deserted during the summer. They flutter about the wall and the windows of the house, I believe with a secret hope of finding a cocoa-nut waiting for them. Large flocks of Starlings, Sparrows and Finches are scouring the stubble and grass fields, now, they will soon

'Under a dark, red-fruited
yew-tree's shade.'
M. Arnold.

"That autumn eve was stilled.
A last remains of sunset dimly burned
O'er the far forests,— like a torch-flame turned
By the wind back upon it's bearer's hand
In one long flare of crimson; as a brand;
The woods beneath lay black ."
'Sordello' R. Browning

Fruit of
Wild Cornel or Dogwood (*Cornus sanguinea*)

Crab·Apple (*Pyrus malus*) and Sloe (*Prunus communis*)

147.

Fruit
of
Wild Service Tree
(Pyrus Torminalis)

October

Oct 21. be joined by the Redwings and Field fares. We have had another week of warm, rainy weather.

25 I was shown some wonderfully fine specimens of the Parasol Fungus today, pale fawn, flecked and shaded with darker tones of the same colour.

31. Mild and damp, with one or two gleams of sunshine. The weather throughout the whole of October, has been very mild

Fruit of Hawthorn
(Crataegus oxycantha)

October

'Now Autumn's fire burns slowly along the woods,
And day by day the dead leaves fall and melt,
And night by night the monitory blast
Wails in the key-hole, telling how it pass'd
O'er empty fields, or upland solitudes,
Or grim, wide wave, and now the power is felt
Of melancholy, tenderer in it's moods,
Than any joy indulgent summer dealt.'

William Allingham.

'O all wide places, far from feverous towns!
Great shining seas! pine-forests! mountains wild!
Rock-bosomed shores! Rough heaths, and sheep-cropt
downs!
Vast pallid clouds! blue spaces undefiled!
Room! give me room! give loneliness and air!
Free things and plenteous in your regions fair.

O God of mountains, stars and boundless spaces!
O God of freedom and of joyous hearts!
When thy face looketh forth from all men's faces;
There will be room enough in crowded marts:
Brood thou around me, and the noise is o'er;
Thy universe my closet with shut door.'

George Macdonald.

Leaves of Sycamore (*Acer-pseudo platanus*)
and Small Maple (*Acer-pseudo campestris*)

NOVEMBER

The ninth month of the old Roman year, which
  began with March. The 11th of November was
  held to mark the beginning of Winter.
The Anglo-Saxon name for November was 'Blot-
  monath'; (Blood-month) the latter name probably
  alluding to the custom of slaughtering cattle
  about Martinmas for winter consumption.

(Enc. Brit.)

Saint's Days.
  - Nov. 1. All Saints' Day
  - Nov. 2. All Souls' Day
  - Nov. 11. St. Martin's
  - Nov. 22 St. Cecelia's
  - Nov. 25. St. Catherine's
  - Nov. 30. St. Andrew's

Mottoes.
  'November take flail,
   Let no ships sail!'

'If there's ice in November that will bear a duck,
  There'll be nothing after, but sludge & muck.'

November

'These early November hours
That crimson the creeper's leaf across
Like a splash of blood, intense, abrupt,
O'er a shield; else gold from rim to boss
And lay it for show on the fairy-cupped
Elf-needled mat of moss.'

R. Browning.

The year lies dying in this evening light;
The poet musing in autumnal woods;
Hears melancholy sighs
Among the withered leaves.

Not so - but like a spirit glorified
The angel of the year departs, lays down
His robes, once green in spring
Or bright with summer's blue;

And having done his mission on the earth,
Filling ten thousand vales with rosy corn,
Orchards with rosy fruit,
And scattering flowers around,—

He lingers for a moment in the west,
With the declining sun sheds over all
A pleasant, fare-well smile
And so returns to God.'

from the German

November

Starling
(sternus vulgaris)

November

1. Steady drizzle of rain, — a regular November day.

3. Cold and foggy in the morning, bright sunshine later. I brought home a little book on British Toad-stools today, with photographs of 65 different varieties. I was disappointed not to find my beau=tiful scarlet, spotted toad-stool among them. In the afternoon I went to the Violet-wood to see how many different kinds I could discover. It was quite hot in the sun, and the autumn foliage looked beautiful in the warm afternoon light. In about half an hours 'time I found 10 different species of fungus, growing in the wood and adjoining field. — all brown in colour, with the exception of two, — One of these was the common Sulphur-tuft, — a rich orange and yellow, this kind is found growing plentifully among dead wood, the other was dull pink above, and a beautiful pale helio=trope beneath. I only found one clump of these; — one or two of them very large in size. There are some interesting notes at the end of the Toad-stool book ; one of which describes the formation of the Toad-stools and Mushroom plants. 'The plant itself is composed of a number of minute threads, which run in all directions under-ground; — and it is only when the plant growing in the ground, becomes vigorous enough to produce seeds or spores that Mushrooms appear. It will thus be seen that the Mushroom, the sole function of which is to produce spores is only the fruit of the Mushroom plant.'

In another note the author states, that there are great numbers of British Toadstools which are edible and which are exceedingly nutritious as an article of diet but in Britain the Mushroom is almost the only fungus eaten; althou abroad Toad-stools are eaten in great quantities.

10. A cold, bright day, after two days of wind and rain and a great gale from the North-west on Thursday. Went out Fungi-hunting again; I went through the meadows this time, I came upon the stumps of two old trees on the

Common
Polyporus
(Polyporus versicolor

The Sulphur-tuft
(agaricus fascicularis)

Stag's Horn
Fungi.

November

10. bank of a field, completely covered with masses of a large flat toad-stool, orange-brown above, with light yellow gills, and scarcely any stem. Under some Beech and Pine trees in another part of the same field, I found a great number of the purple-gilled variety; some of the larger ones were quite dull brown in colour, evidently only the young, new toad-stools have the beautiful heliotrope tint beneath. I found a very handsome species growing in tiers up the trunk of a Beech tree, where the bark had been torn away. It was dark blue-black above, and pure white below, - the gills being curiously waved and corruscated, - giving them the effect of white coral. In the open part of the meadow I found several other species, - one with a shiny, brown top, like a bun, and farther on in a little wood, I gathered some of the Common Polyporus from the side of a rotten stump; and a delicate little Stag's Horn Fungi or Claveria. The pale yellow fronds of Bracken looked very pretty in the wood, growing among the dark Bramble leaves. The road was quite yellow in places with fallen Elm leaves. One or two sharp frosts would strip the trees bare, although many of the leaves are still quite green.

13. Went for an early morning walk across the fields to Elmdon Lane to make some sketches of a Blackbird and Thrush at a cottage there. It was a grey, perfectly still morning with a slight fog, that veiled the distant woods and trees in a purple mist. Many of the trees were quite bare, but the Oaks still have their foliage and were all shades of bronze and brown, the hedges and banks too were glowing with the golden tints of Nut leaves and Bracken, and everywhere there was a delicious autumn scent of fallen leaves. I passed through one grass field where there quantities of toad-stools of all kinds. It was curious that though I had crossed several other grass fields, I did'nt see a single toad-stool, till I came to this one.

Green Woodpecker
(Gecinus viridis)

NOVEMBER

'O Wild West Wind, thou breath of Autumn's being,
  Thou, from whose unseen presence the leaves dead
  Are driven like ghosts from an enchanter fleeing,

Yellow and black, and pale, and hectic red,
  Pestilence-stricken multitudes! O thou
  Who chariotest to their dark wintry bed

The wingèd seeds, where they lie cold and low,
  Each like a corpse within it's grave, until
  Thine azure sister of the Spring shall blow

Her chariot o'er the dreaming earth, and fill
  (Driving sweet buds like flocks to feed in air)
  With living hues and odours, plain and hill;

Wild Spirit, which art moving everywhere,
  Destroyer and preserver; hear, oh hear!

Make me thy lyre, even as the forest is,
  What if my leaves are falling like it's own?
  The tumult of thy mighty harmonies

Will take from both a deep autumnal tone,
  Sweet though in sadness, Be thou, Spirit fierce,
  My spirit! Be thou me, impetuous one!

Drive my dead thoughts over the universe,
  Like withered leaves, to quicken a new birth;
  And by the incantation of this verse,

Scatter, as from an unextinguished hearth
  Ashes and sparks, my words among mankind!
  Be through my lips to unawakened earth

The trumpet of a prophesy! O Wind,
  If Winter comes, can Spring be far behind?'

Shelley

Bramble leaves

NOVEMBER

13. The wife of a game-keeper living next door to the cottage where I was painting the birds, showed me two fine, stuffed specimens of Night-jars, which her husband had shot in the neighbourhood. I have often seen these birds on Dartmoor and on the Surrey Commons and in Cumberland, but I did not know before they were to be found in this part of the country.

14. I saw a Kingfisher fly across the little pool by the road-side below Olton station today. The new Catkins are showing on all the Alder and Hazel trees now.
The sun had a most remarkable appearance just before setting tonight. I never saw it look so large in my life. It was deep crimson, shaded with purple which gave it a globular appearance, and it looked like a huge fire-balloon suspended against a curtain of grey cloud.

15. Stormy day with a gale of wind and rain from the West. I walked home from Solihull in the after-noon All the way along, the leaves were whirling down from the trees in hundreds and dancing along the road before me.

19. The first sharp white frost we have had; cold North-west wind with showers of hail and rain.

26. Cycled to Solihull; and back through the lanes past the Oak woods. The sun was shining brightly, lighting up the dying fronds of Bracken among the under-growth, and the scanty foliage on the half bare Oak trees. The leaves lay thick all along the way. I heard a Thrush singing most sweetly in the big Beech tree at the top of Kineton Lane.

30. North-west wind, with showers of rain.

162.

Seed-vessels
of
Rose-bay Willow-herb

Sing on sweet thrush, upon the leafless bough,
Sing on sweet bird, I listen to thy strain,
And agèd Winter, mid his early reign,
At thy blythe carol, clears his furrowed brow.'
                                        Burns.

Song Thrush
(Turdus musicus)

Like as the thrush in winter, when the skies
Are drear and dark, and all the woods are bare,
Sings undismayed, till from his melodies
Odours of spring float through the frozen air,—
So in my heart when sorrow's icy breath
Is bleak and bitter and its frost is strong,
Leaps up, defiant of despair and death
A sunlit fountain of triumphant song.
Sing on sweet singer till the violets come
And south winds blow, sing on prophetic bird!
O if my lips, which are for ever dumb
Could sing to men what my sad heart has heard
Life's darkest hour with songs of joy would ring,
Life's blackest frost would blossom into Spring

Edmond Holmes

Seed-vessels
of
Cow-Parsnep.
and
Beaked Parsley

166.

Nipple-wort
and
Dock

' When all aloud the wind doth blow,
And coughing drowns the parson's saw,
And birds sit brooding in the snow,
And Marion's nose looks red and raw. '

Shakespere.

DECEMBER

December was the last month of the old Roman year
which was divided into ten months.
The Saxons called it 'winter-monat' or winter month,
and 'heligh-monat', or holy month, from the fact
that Christmas fell within it. The 22nd of Dec-
-ember is the date of the winter solstice, when
the sun reaches the tropic of Capricorn.

Saints Days etc.

    Dec. 25. Christmas Day
    Dec. 29. St 'Thomas' Day
    Dec. 31. New Year's Eve.

Mottoes

    'Bounce buckram velvets dear,
    Christmas comes but once a year,
    When it comes it brings good cheer,
    And when it's gone, it's never near.'

    'In December keep yourself warm and sleep.'

    'A green Yule, makes a fat kirk-yard.'

December

'And after him came next the chill December,
Yet he, through merry feasting which he made
And great bon-fires, did not the cold remember;
His Saviours birth his mind so much did glad;
Upon a shaggy-bearded goat he rode,
The same wherewith Dan Jove in tender yeares;
They say, was nourisht by th' Iaean Mayd;
And in his hand a broad, deep bowl he beares,
Of which he freely drinks an health to all his peere
                                        Spenser.

'A wrinkled crabbèd man they picture thee,
  Old Winter, with a rugged beard as grey
  As the long moss upon the apple-tree;
 Blue-lipt, an ice drop at thy sharp blue nose,
 Close muffled up, and on thy dreary way
 Plodding alone through sleet and drifting snows.
 They should have drawn thee by the high-heapt hearth
 Old Winter! seated in thy great armed chair;
 Watching the children at their Christmas mirth;
 Or circled by them as thy lips declare
 Some merry jest, or tale of murder dire,

  Or troubled spirit that disturbs the night;
  Pausing at times to rouse the smouldering fire,
  Or taste the old October brown and bright.
                                        R. Southey.

Berries
of
Privet (*Ligustrum vulgare*)
and
Holly (*Ilex aquifolium*)

December

Dec. 1. Very bright and clear with a cold wind from the north east. For many weeks past the birds have been coming to be fed in the mornings. Today I put out a cocoa-nut,—to the great joy of the Tom-tits; numbers of them were pecking away at it all through the day,—mostly Blue-tits.

4. Three days of rain, wind and sunshine.

7. Hard white frost and fog. This is the first real winter's day we have had. Crowds of birds came to be fed this morning; There were great battles among the Tits over the cocoa-nut, and once a Robin got right into it, and refused to let the Tits approach, until he had had all he wanted.

I don't think the Robins really care for cocoa-nut; but they don't like to see the Tits enjoying anything, without claiming a share

9 We woke up to a storm of whirling snowflakes this morning,—the first snow this winter. The storm was soon over however and it was followed by bright sunshine and a sharp frost at night.

10. Cold, frosty day. It seems as if winter had begun in earnest; but the fore-casts prophecy a speedy change.

12 Wind and rain with bright intervals. There was a most beautiful rain-bow visible in the morning for about ten minutes.

14 Heavy fall of snow.

20 After a rapid thaw and four days of wonderfully mild, still weather, without wind or rain; the wind has gone round to the east and it looks as if we might have a frosty Christmas after all.

25. We woke to a snowy Christmas morning; sunshine later and sharp frost at night.

26 Another heavy fall of snow in the night.

"Amid the leafless thorn
 the merry Wren,
When icicles hang dripping
 from the rock,
Pipes her perennial lay;
Even when the flakes
 Broad on her pinions fall,
She lightly flies
Athwart the shower
 and sings upon the wing."

James Graham.

Wren
(Sylvia troglodytes)
and
Hedge Sparrow
(Accentor modulares)

DECEMBER

'A naked house, a naked moor,
A shivering pool before the door,
A garden bare of flowers or fruit
And poplars at the garden foot.
Such is the place that I live in,
Bleak without and bare within.

Yet shall your ragged moor receive
The incomparable pomp of eve,
And the gold glories of the dawn
Behind your shivering trees be drawn;
And when the wind from place to place,
Doth the unmoored cloud-galleons chase;
Your garden gloom and gleam again
With leaping sun, with glancing rain.
Here shall the wizard moon ascend
The heavens, in the crimson end
Of day's declining splendour; here
The army of the stars appear:
The neighbouring hollows dry and wet
Spring shall with tender flowers beset,
And oft the morning muses see
Larks rising from the broomy lea;
And every fairy wheel and thread
Of cobweb dew-bediamonded.
When daisies go, shall winter time
Silver the simple grass with rime.
Autumnal frost enchant the pool
And make the cart-ruts beautiful,
And when snow-bright the moor expands
How shall your children clap their hands:
To make this Earth our hermitage
A cheerful and a changeful page
God's bright and intricate device
Of days and seasons doth suffice.'

R.L. Stevenson.

'It's verdure trails
the Ivy shoot
Along the ground
from root to root ;
Or climbing high
With random maze,
O'er elm, and ash and alder strays,
And round each trunk
A net-work weaves,
Fantastic, and each bough with leaves
Of countless shapes, entwines and studs
With pale green blooms
And half formed buds.
The Ivy, of our native flowers
That now among the latest pours
It's pale green bloom, and ripes it's seed
Of black and shining balls to feed,
Impervious to the winter's frost,
The little bird's afflicted host;
The Ivy, fairest plant to seize
And promptest on the neighbouring trees
O'er bole and branch with leaves that shine
All glossy bright, tenacious twine
And the else naked woodland scene
Clothe with a raiment
Fresh and green.'
                    Bishop Mant

Common Ivy
(Hedera Hélix)

December

27. In the paper today it reports that all Britain lies under snow from John o' Groats to Land's End for the first time for six years.

28. Bright and clear, more heavy snow storms are reported from all parts of the country, accompanied in some places by thunder and lightning. Skating has commenced in the fens.

30 The frost still holds, Snow lightly throughout the day. The birds have become wonderfully bold this last week since their usual hunting grounds have been buried in snow. The Blackbirds and Thrushes are usually rather shy, and fly away at the approach of any one, but now, they only hop away to a little distance and sit watching with their bright eyes, from beneath the friendly shelter of a bush, waiting to go back to their feast of crumbs. The Tits and Robins and Sparrows scarcely take any notice of one. I have noticed Chaffinches feeding among the other birds the last few days, they seldom come to feed; though in the Spring they are often to be seen on the lawn, busily engaged in picking out the moss from the turf, for their nests.

31. Hogmonay, There is a rise in the temperature this morning, the wind has gone round to the South west; and there is every sign of an approaching thaw. The papers report more falls of snow, Out-lying farms and villages in Yorkshire, East Lothian, and the Highlands are entirely isolated by the deep snow.

Mistletoe
(Viscus album)

Wild Flowers found in the neighbourhood of Olton, Warwickshire.

Alder. ····· Alnus glutinosa
Agrimony (Common)···Agrimonia eupatoria
Agrimony (Hemp)····· Eupatorium cannabinum
Angelica (Wild)···Angelica sylvestris
Anemone (Wood)···Anemone membrosa
Apple (Crab) ···· Pyrus malus
Ash (Common)····· Praxinus excelsior
Ash (Mountain)···Pyrus aucuparia
Avens (Common)···Geum urbinus
Bedstraw (Yellow)···· Galium verum
Bedstraw (Cross-wort)··Galium boreale
Beech ······ Fagus sylvatica
Bell·flower (Giant)···Campanula persicifolia
Betony (Wood)···· Stachys Belonica
Bilberry ····Vacoinum myrtilis
Bind·weed (Small)···Convolvulus arvenis
Bind·weed (Greater)··· Convolvulus sepium
Bartsia (Red) ······Bartsia odontites
Blackberry or Bramble···Rubus fruticosus
Blackthorn or Sloe····· Prunus communis
Brooklime·······Veronica becca-bunge
Broom ············· Sarothamnus scopareus
Bryony (Black)·····Tamus communis
Bugle (Common)····· Ajuga reptans
Buckwheat (Common)·Polygonum bistorta
Buckwheat (Climbing)··Polygonum convolvulus
Bullace ·········· Prunus communis
Burdock (Common)·· Arctium lappa
Burnet (Great)····· Sanguisorba officinalis

Bur-reed (Branched)···· Sparganium ramosum
Bur-reed (Unbranched)··· Sparganium simplex
Buttercup (Meadow)··· Ranunculous acris
Buttercup (Creeping)··· Ranunculous reptans
Buttercup (Bulbous)····· Ranunculous bulbosus
Campion (Red)····· Lychnis diurna
Campion (White)····· Lychnis vespertina
Campion (Bladder)····· Silene inflata
Celandine (Lesser)····· Ranunculous fiscaria
Celandine (Greater)····· Chelidonium majus
Centaury (Common)···· Erythraea centaurium
Chesnut (Horse)····· Aesculus Hippocastanum
Chesnut (Spanish or Sweet)·· Castanea vesca
Cherry (Wild)······· Prunus avium
Chickweed········ Stellaria media
Clover (Purple)····· Trifolium pratense
Clover (White or Dutch)···· Trifolium repans
Cinquefoil (Creeping)···· Potentilla reptans
Cinquefoil (Strawberry-leaved) Potentilla fragariastrum
Cinquefoil (Purple Marsh)···· Comarum palustre
Colt's Foot ······ Tussilogo farfara
Cornel or Dogwood····· Cornus sanguinea
Cowslip ······ Primula veris
Crowfoot (Water)······ Ranunculous aquatilis
Crowfoot (Corn)····· Ranunculous arvensis
Crowfoot (Wood)····· Ranunculous auricomus
Crowfoot (Celery-leaved)··· Ranunculous sceleratus
Cranes-bill (Meadow)····· Geranium pratense
Cranes-bill (Doves-foot)···· Geranium molle
Cranes-bill (Dusky)····· Geranium phaeum
Comfrey (Common)···· Symphytum officinale
Cress (Water)····· Nasturtium officinale
Cress (Large-flowered Bitter)··· Cardamine amara
Cress (Yellow Bitter)··· Nasturtium amphibium
Cress (Hairy Bitter)···· Cardamine hirsuta
Cow Parsnep ···· Heraclum spondilium
Cuckoo Flower or Ladies Smock·· Cardamine pratensis

Cuckoo Pint, Wild Arum or Lords & Ladies ... Arum maculatum
Daisy (Common) .... Bellis perennis
Daisy (Com) .... Chrysanthemum leucanthemum
Daffodil .... Narcissus pseudo-narcissus
Dandelion .... Leontodon tarascacum
Dock (Broad-leaved) ... Rumex pulcher
Dock (Curled) .... Rumex cuspus
Flowering Rush .... Butum umbellatus
Figwort (Knotted) ..... Scrophularia nodosa
Forgetmenot (Large Water) .. Myosotis palustris
Forgetmenot (Small Water) . Myosotis caespitosa
Foxglove .... Digitalis purpurea
Fumitory (Common) ..... Fumaria officinale
Gorse or Whin .... Ulex Europaeus
Garlic (Broad-leaved) ... Allum ursinum
Germander (Wood) ...... Teucrum Ocorodonia
Golden Rod .... Solidaga vulgaris
Goat's Beard .... Tragopogon pratensis
Goose-Grass or Cleavers ... Galium aparine
Hazel Nut .... Corylus avellana
Hawthorn or May .... Crataegus oxycantha
Hawk's-bit (Rough) .... Aspargia hispeda
Hawkweed (Mouse Ear) .. Hieracum pilosella
Heather or Ling .... Calluna vulgaris
Hare-bell .... Campanula rotundifolia
Heartsease (Yellow) ... Viola tricolor
Herb Robert or Wild Geranium .. Geranium Robertianium
Hemlock (Common) ...... Conium maculatum
Hemp nettle .... Galeopsis Tetrahil
Holly .... Ilex aquifolium
Honeysuckle .... Lonicera caprifolium
Hyacinth or Blue-bell ... Agraphis nutans
Iris (Yellow) .... Iris pseudo-acoris
Ivy (Common) .... Hedera helix
Knapweed (Black or Discoid) .. Centauria nigra
Knautia (Field) .... Polygonum
Knot-grass .... Polygonum arvensis

Lady's Mantle	Alchemilla vulgaris
Lime	Tilea Europaea
Lily of the Valley	Convallaria majalis
Lettuce (Ivy-leaved)	Lactuca muralis
Loose-strife (Purple)	Lythrum salicaria
Loose-strife (Creeping)	Lysimachea numularia
Louse-wort (Pasture)	Pedicularis sylvatica
Madder (Blue Field)	Sherardia arvensis
Mallow (Common)	Malva sylvestris
Mallow (Musk)	Malva moschata
Maple (Small)	Acer pseudo-campestris
Marsh Marigold	Caltha palustris
Mayweed (Scentless)	Matricaria inodora
Meadow Sweet	Spirea salicifolea
Meddick (Black)	Medicago lupulina
Milkwort	Polygala vulgaris
Mint (Water)	Mentha aquatica
Mint (Corn)	Mentha arvensis
Meadow Saffron	Colchicum autumnale
Mistletoe	Viscum album
Moschatel (Tuberous)	Adoxa moschatellina
Mullein (Great)	Verbascum thapsus
Mustard (Common Hedge)	Sysymbrium officinale
Nettle (White Dead)	Lamium album
Nettle (Red Dead)	Lamium purpureum
Nettle (Stinging)	Urtica diorea
Night-shade (Woody) or Bittersweet	Solanum dulcanera
Night-shade (Enchanter's)	Circæa lutetiana
Nipple-wort (Common)	Lapsana communis
Oak	Quercus robur
Orchis (Early Purple)	Orchis mascula
Orchis (Spotted Palmate)	Orchis maculata
Ox-slip	Primula elatior
Parsley (Wild Beaked)	Anthriscus sylvestris
Pear (Wild)	Pyrus communis
Periwinkle (Lesser)	Vinca minor
Persicaria (Spotted)	Polygonum persicarea
Pimpernel (Scarlet)	Anagallis arvensis

Pimpernel (Yellow)	Lysimachia memorum
Pine or Scotch Fir	Pinus sylvestris
Plantain (Great Water)	Alisma plantago
Plantain (Greater)	Plantago major
Plantain (Ribwort)	Plantago lanceolata
Poppy (Scarlet)	Papaver Rhoeas
Primrose	Primula vulgaris
Privet	Ligustrum vulgare
Ragged Robin	Lychnis flos-cuculi
Ragwort (Common)	Senecio Jacobaea
Raspberry	Rubus idaeus
Rattle (Yellow)	Rhinanthus cristi
Rose (Dog)	Rosa canina
Rose (Trailing)	Rosa arvensis
Saxifrage (White Meadow)	Saxifragia granulis
Scorpion Grass (Field)	Myosotis arvensis
Sanicle (Wood)	Sanicula Europaea
Scabious (Devil's-bit)	Scabiosa succisa
Self-heal	Prunella vulgaris
Service-tree (Wild)	Pyrus terminalis
Skull-cap	Scutelleria galericulata
Shepherd's Purse	Capsella bursa pastoris
Silver Weed	Potentilla anserina
Smooth Heath Bedstraw	Galium saxatile
Sorrel (Common)	Rumex acetosa
Sorrel (Sheep's)	Rumex acetosella
Sow Thistle	Sonchus palustris
Spearwort (Lesser)	Ranunculous flammula
Speedwell (Germander)	Veronica chamaedris
Speedwell (Common)	Veronica officinalis
Speedwell (Procumbent Field)	Veronica agrestis
Spurry (Corn)	Spergula arvensis
Stitchwort (Greater)	Stellaria holostea
Stitchwort (Lesser)	Stellaria graminea
St. John's Wort (Small Upright)	Hypericum pulchrum
St. John's Wort (Perforated)	Hypericum perforatum
Strawberry (Wild)	Fragara vesca
Stone-crop (English)	Sedum anglicum
Poplar (Black)	Populus nigra

Tare (Slender)	Vicia tetrasperma
Tansy (Common)	Tanacetum vulgare
Thistle (Cotton)	Onopordum arcanthium
Thistle (Creeping Plume)	Cnicus arvensis
Thistle (Welted)	Carduus acanthoides
Thyme	Thymus serpyllum
Toad-flax (Yellow)	Linaria vulgaris
Toad-flax (Ivy-leaved)	Linaria cymbalaria
Tormentil	Potentilla tormentilla
Treacle Mustard	Erysimum Alliaria
Trefoil (Greater Bird's-foot)	Lotus major
Trefoil (Lesser Bird's-foot)	Lotus corniculatus
Twayblade	Listera ovata
Valerian (Marsh)	Valeriana dioecca
Valerian (Great Wild)	Valeriana officinalis
Vetch (Early Purple)	Orobus tuberosus
Vetch (Bush)	Vicia sepium
Vetch (Purple Tufted)	Vicia cracca
Vetchling (Meadow)	Lathyrus pratensis
Violet (Sweet)	Viola odorata
Violet (Dog)	Viola canina
Water Lily (White)	Nymphoea alba
Water Lily (Yellow)	Nymphoea lutea
Weasel Snout (Yellow)	Galeobdolen luteum
Willow (Goat)	Salix caprea
Willow (Purple)	Salix purpures
Willow Herb (Great Hairy)	Epilobium hirsutum
Willow Herb (Small Hairy)	Epilobium parvi-florum
Willow Herb (Smooth-leaved)	Epilobium montanum
Wood Sorrel	Oxalis acetesella
Woodruff	Asperula odorata
Yew	Taxus baccata
Yarrow (Common) or Milfoil	Achillea millefolium
Yarrow (Sneeze-wort)	Achillea Ptarmica

Wild Birds found in the neighbourhood of Olton, Warwickshire.

Blackbird or Merle	Turdus merula
Blackcap Warbler	Sylvia atricapilla
Bullfinch	Loxia pyrrhula
Bunting (Black-headed or Reed)	Emberiza schoeniculus
Bunting (Yellow) or Yellowhammer	Emberiza citrinella
Bunting (Common)	Emberiza milaria
Chaffinch	Fringilla coelebs
Chiff-chaff	Sylvia hippolais
Corn Crake or Landrail	Ortygometra crex
Coot	Fulica atra
Crow (Carrion)	Corvus corone
Cuckoo	Cuculus canorus
Dab-chick or Little Grebe	Podiceps minor
Fieldfare	Turdus pilaris
Fly-catcher (Spotted)	Muscicapa gresola
Goldfinch	Carduelis elegans
Golden-crested Wren	Regulus cristatus
Greenfinch	Coccothraustes chloris
Hawfinch or Grosbeak	Cocothraustes vulgaris
Hedge Accentor or Hedge Sparrow	Accentor modularis
Heron	Ardea cineria
Jackdaw	Corvus monedula
Jay	Garrulus glandarius
Kestrel	Tinnunculus Alaudarius
Kingfisher	Alcedo ispeda
Lark (Sky) or Laverock	Alauda arvensis
Lark (Wood)	Alauda arborea
Martin (House)	Hirundo urbica
Martin (Sand)	Hirundo riparia
Magpie	Pica caudata
Mallard or Wild Duck	Anas boschas
Moor-hen or Water-hen	Gallinula chloropus
Linnet	Linaria cannabina

Nightjar or Goatsucker	Caprimuleus Europæus
Nightingale	Philomela luscinia
Nuthatch	Sitta Europæa
Owl (White, Barn or Screech)	Strix flammea
Partridge	Perdrix cinereus
Pheasant	Phasianus Colchicus
Pipit (Meadow)	Anthus pratensis
Pipit (Tree)	Anthus arboreus
Redwing	Turdus iliacus
Ring Ouzel	Turdus torquatus
Robin or Redbreast	Sylvia rubecula
Rook	Corvus frugilagus
Sparrow (House)	Passer domesticus
Sparrow-Hawk	Accipiter nisus
Starling	Sternus vulgaris
Shrike (Red-backed)	Lanius collurio
Stone-chat	Sylvia rubicola
Swallow	Hirundo rustica
Swift	Hirundo apus
Thrush (Song)	Turdus musicus
Thrush (Missel)	Turdus viscivorus
Tree-Creeper	Certhia familiaris
Turtle Dove	Turtur auritus
Tit (Great or Ox-eye)	Parus major
Tit (Blue)	Parus cæruleus
Tit (Cole)	Parus ater
Tit (Marsh)	Parus palustris
Tit (Long-tailed)	Parus caudatus
Wagtail (Pied	Motacilla Yarrelli
Wagtail (Grey	Motacilla sulphurea
Wagtail (Yellow)	Matacilla flavia
Whinchat	Sylvia rubetra

Warbler (Garden) . . . . Sylvia hortensis
Warbler (Sedge) . . . . Sylvia salicaria
Warbler (Willow) or Willow Wren . . . . Sylvia trochylus
Warbler (Wood) or Wood Wren . . . Sylvia Sylvicola
White-throat . . . . . . Sylvia cinerea
White-throat (Lesser) . . . . . Sylvia sylviella
Water Rail . . . . Rallus aquaticus
Wood-pecker (Green) . . . . . . Gecinus viridis
Wood Pigeon, Ring Dove or Cushat . . Columba palumbus
Wren . . . . Sylvia troglodytes
Redstart or Fire-tail . . . . Sylvia phœnicurus